Elvin McDonald

Little Plants for Small Spaces

How to select and grow mini plants
and trees indoors and out

M. EVANS AND COMPANY, INC.
New York, New York 10017

A completely revised, updated
and expanded version of
Miniature Plants for Home and Greenhouse

M. Evans and Company titles are distributed in
the United States by the J. B. Lippincott Company,
East Washington Square, Philadelphia, Pa. 19105;
and in Canada by McClelland & Stewart Ltd.,
25 Hollinger Road, Toronto M4B 3G2, Ontario

Library of Congress Cataloging in Publication Data

McDonald, Elvin.
  Little plants for small spaces.

  Includes index.
  1. Miniature plants.   2. Gardening, Miniature.
I. Title.
SB419.M24   1975   635.9   75-15794
ISBN 0-87131-195-X

9 8 7 6 5 4 3 2 1

Contents

Author's Preface		4
1.	Miniature Plants and Their Ways	7
2.	The Perfect Miniature—*Sinningia pusilla*	9
3.	Miniature African Violets	16
4.	Miniature Begonias	26
5.	Miniature Daffodils and Other Little Bulbs for Forcing	38
6.	Miniature Evergreens	46
7.	Miniature Geraniums	50
8.	Miniature and Compact English Ivies	62
9.	Miniature Orchids	71
10.	Miniature Roses	84
11.	A Multitude of Excellent Miniature Plants	93
12.	Gardening with Miniature Plants	170
	Appendix	188
	Index	191

Author's Preface

In this book I have been concerned primarily with true miniature plants that may be cultivated indoors. With just a few exceptions, those discussed here either mature, or may be maintained by pruning and training, at less than 10 inches overall height. Of course, the seedlings of many plants are delightful miniatures during their first months of life, though ultimately they grow to large proportions. Part of the fun of gardening in miniature lies in the discovery of tiny new plants—those at the vanishing point, and up to a few inches tall.

I hope that this book may encourage breeders to develop more miniature plants. Wouldn't it be grand to have thimble-size begonias, geraniums, amaryllis, roses, coleus and calceolarias? There are miniature begonias, geraniums and roses, but mostly they are not such diminutive perfections as *Sinningia pusilla* and its family, described in the second chapter of this book. Many of the hardy calceolarias, described in Chapter 11, are excellent for a cold or cool greenhouse, sun-heated pit or cold frame, but certainly they are not candidates for an apartment or house window sill. I could not make a single entry under amaryllis in this book—and what a shame! There are Amaryllids included, but not miniatures of the popular ones cultivated by most indoor gardeners. Miniature geraniums and orchids come nearest to being top-ranked with *Sinningia pusilla*—and there are literally thousands of miniature cacti and other succulents that deserve consideration. Some of the most noteworthy of these are listed and described in Chapter 11.

When I first wrote this book in 1960 and 1961, I honestly thought there were not enough miniatures available to justify hardcover publication. However, my wise and determined editor, Helen Van Pelt Wilson, kept encouraging my search, and soon I found there were more than enough. In fact, Chapter 11 grew so large it had to be encoded with numbers which you can decode by using the chart at the end of the chapter. The plants in Chapter 11, along with the miniature roses, bulbs and evergreens treated separately, take this book far beyond its original title, *Miniature Plants for Home and Greenhouse*, for in fact this book includes hundreds of winter-hardy plants for the making of mini gardens outdoors as well as inside.

Now, some thirty books later, it has been a trip of pleasant nostalgia to go back to my first. I have been amazed that the little plants I was growing at the time, both in the suburbs of Long Island and Kansas City, have flashed back so vividly in my memory that I really feel I should get up from my typewriter and go see if they need a drink of water or a little pruning. That precious silver orchid, described in Chapter 1, was frozen one below-zero night in Missouri when my greenhouse heater went on the fritz, but I will never forget that special plant and how I treasured it. Or those tiny English ivies and satin-and-silk begonia babies my friend Vera Dillard shared so generously with me. I don't know that I talk to my plants, but looking back, I can say quite soberly that I have been communicating with them all of my life.

Today I live in an apartment in midtown Manhattan where I grow more than 300 plants in sunny windows and under fluorescent lights. In addition, I have an acre in Southampton, near the eastern tip of Long Island, where I garden as much as possible—meaning I try to limit my acquisitions and plantings so that their care is always a pleasure. Years ago I vowed never again to be one of those wild-eyed and sweaty gardeners who has lost sight of what it is all about. Sometimes I travel so much I think the most appropriate garden for me would be a mini greenhouse scaled to fit under the jet seat in front of me, and then I could just carry my garden wherever I go.

The original *Miniature Plants for Home and Greenhouse* enjoyed reasonable success through the usual distribution of hardcover books in local shops and as a Selection of the American Garden Guild Book Club. At some point dollhouse collectors discovered it as a guide for selecting living plants small enough to be used in realistic Lilliputian roomsettings. Then it was declared out of print and for several years even I, the author, did not have a copy. Early in 1974 with the all-encompassing rage for gardening in general and house plants in particular full upon us, my editor at Popular Library, Sheila Levine, asked me if I would revise the original for a new paperback under the title *Little Plants for Small Spaces*. Now, approximately a year after publication of that edition, with more than 100,000 copies in print, it has been my pleasure to make slight revisions and updatings once again for a hardcover edition which I am especially proud—and satisfied—to have published by M. Evans and Company, whose president, George De Kay, and I have produced some seventeen books for the Hearst Corporation (the 16-volume *Good Housekeeping Illustrated Encyclopedia of Gardening* and the single volume *Good Housekeeping Basic Gardening Techniques*), but this is our first effort under the imprint of M. Evans.

Two dear friends in Kansas City helped most in the creation of this book as it was published originally, Kathleen Bourke and Vera Dillard—and in special thanks, I dedicate this new edition to them. For help with the updating and expansion, I want to thank Michael Kartuz and his marvelous mother; Ellie Bogen for her expertise with African violets; Ralph Moore and Ernest Williams for miniature roses; Joy Logee Martin and Mary Ellen Ross for begonias and geraniums; Bess Shippy for English ivies; Jean Merkel and Charles Marden Fitch for orchids; my childhood pen pal, now the curator of bamboos at the Smithsonian, Dr. Thomas Soderstrom, for help with Chapter 11; and Elaine Brix for typing the new manuscript.

Elvin McDonald

New York City and
Southampton, New York
May, 1975

1. Miniature Plants and Their Ways

The searching out of miniature plants is one of the most fascinating aspects of gardening that I have tried. Growing and observing miniature plants is a more intimate experience than dealing with large plants. In a way, it is like viewing a precious object through a microscope.

For the plant hobbyist, miniatures make it possible to have a wide variety in a small amount of space. Take, for example, the person who admires and likes to collect African violets. Six to ten regular-size plants may completely engulf the space of an average window. But with miniatures, this same space could easily accommodate two dozen or more plants, each a different variety. This same idea applies to orchids, geraniums, begonias, cacti and other succulents and, for that matter, to all of the plants discussed in this book.

Some miniature plants occur in nature—*Sinningia pusilla*, for example. Others, such as Peperomia 'Pixie' and *Hedera helix* 'Needlepoint' have occurred in cultivation as mutations. And still others like Begonia 'China Doll' and *Sinningia* 'Coral Baby' are the result of hybridizing programs for the development of miniature plants.

Opportunities with miniatures are boundless. They are delightful in individual containers. Perhaps their forte is use

7

in miniature gardens and landscapes. Planting may be a bowl just a few inches in diameter, or it could be two feet or more square, or rectangular, and designed with tiny paths, a brook and a footbridge.

One of the greatest assets of a miniature is its ability to be grown in a situation that would be impossible for a large plant. For example, say that yours is a small, crowded window in a city apartment. The atmosphere is arid in fall and winter, and the light poor. Few really attractive plants of regular size would do well. But, fill a terrarium with shade-loving miniatures, cover it with a piece of clear glass, and you have an opportunity to grow perfect miniature plants. Or put a fluorescent light over your tiny garden and you can have it on a bookcase shelf in the darkest part of the house.

As a gardener, you can do everything with miniature plants. Although emphasis in this book is placed on miniature plants for indoors, they are indispensable out of doors. Some are hardy even in cold winters, others are tender and should be brought inside during the months of freezing temperatures. Although my outdoor garden contains hundreds of different plants, among my favorites are the miniature, needle-bearing conifers (evergreens). They grow slowly and sturdily, require little of my time, yet in beauty they are invaluable. The planting I made last year will look very much the same fifteen years from now, yet each tree will improve in appearance as it grows little by little through the seasons to come.

When you collect miniature plants indoors, there is always something just ahead that will be even more interesting than what you have grown before. After the chapter on miniature orchids was completed, I found another jewel, *Erythroides nobilis argyrocentrum*. Sometimes called the silver orchid, it is for foliage that this plant is cultivated. The glistening, satiny leaves of green have a striking silver network. In midwinter it sends up a small spike of white flowers. My erythroides thrives in a closed terrarium in low-light intensity (under fluorescent lights, about 18 inches from the tubes). This orchid likes high humidity at all times, and temperatures between 60 and 75 degrees. Grow it in moist osmunda.

2. The Perfect Miniature— Sinningia pusilla

The smallest tropical plant I know has still another distinction—it is also the "bloomingest"! Commonly known as the miniature gloxinia, *Sinningia pusilla* is to me Lilliputian perfection among tiny plants to grow indoors. It is a gesneriad with beautiful foliage, a constant uplifting of lavender flowers, and it is available to anyone willing to part with a dollar.

This plant looks overpotted even in a 2¼-inch pot. It grows in correct proportion to a true thumb-size container, a small thumb at that. The 1¼-inch plastic pots available today make containers of just the right dimensions, both culturally and esthetically for *Sinningia pusilla*. I have seen it grown to equal beauty in a thimble.

Pusilla has oval, olive-green leaves which have a distinct network of reddish brown veins. These grow in a rosette from a tiny, fleshy tuber. The five-petaled, lavender flowers rise about an inch high on wiry stems. They are lined with a darker shade of violet. Throats are white, creamy white, or sometimes even palest yellow. Aside from the fact that this plant flowers almost continuously, without resting, it is also resistant to bud blast, a condition that can be bothersome with other kinds of gloxinias. In a moist atmosphere (45 per cent or more humidity) with a temperature range of 65 to 75 degrees F., each flower of *Sinningia pusilla* lasts seven days or longer.

🐿 Growing Medium

Any growing medium that has been used successfully for African violets or gloxinias is suitable for *Sinningia pusilla*, that is, it should contain humus, retain moisture but be well drained. Michael Kartuz, one of the most successful growers, recommends specifically his G-B-S Growing Mix (Gesneriad-Begonia-Saintpaulia). This is a soilless mix which you can order by mail from Mr. Kartuz (see the list of suppliers at the back of the book), or you can mix your own following his recipe:

> 6 quarts sphagnum peat moss, screened
> 4 quarts Terralite vermiculite
> 4 quarts coarse perlite
> 2 tablespoons ground limestone
> 1 quart (approximately) warm water

Put all the ingredients in a suitable container, for example a clean plastic garbage pail, and mix well. The medium is ready to use immediately, or you can store it indefinitely in a plastic bag. (Incidentally, a 5-inch pot holds approximately 1 quart.) Mr. Kartuz recommends that the peat moss be rubbed through a half-inch mesh hardware cloth sieve to remove lumps and small twigs. Canadian or European peat moss is satisfactory. It should be light brown in color when dry and very spongy. Do not use Michigan or sedge peat.

Keep the soil in which Sinningia pusilla is growing nicely moist at all times. Monthly feedings of house-plant fertilizer, mixed to half the strength of package recommendations, will keep pusilla in constant bloom.

As with any plant that blooms continuously, it is important to keep old flowers and leaves clipped. Otherwise, in a humid

ILLUSTRATION 1. Sinningia pusilla, *surrounded by its family of little gloxinias. Upper row, left to right, 'Snowflake,' 'Patty Ann,' 'Poupee.' Lower row, 'White Sprite,'* S. pusilla *and 'Bright Eyes.' (Scale: 2-inch pots.)*

atmosphere, they may fall on new foliage or buds and cause rotting. Pusilla has such a small root system that if you attempt to pull or jerk old flower stems from the plant, you will separate it from the tuber. It is therefore best to clip off old blooms and leaves with small scissors. Cut flower stems as close as possible to the point of origin.

🌿 From Seeds

Pusilla is now available from many sources, either as a plant or seeds. Seeds should be sown on a sieved and sterilized growing medium, such as milled sphagnum moss. They are sprinkled over the moistened medium, but not covered. Place the container in which seeds are sown in a polyethylene bag to conserve moisture and set in a warm (70–72 degrees F.), shady spot—perhaps on top of a kitchen cabinet or on the propagating bench of your greenhouse. After seeds germinate and growth starts, the protective cover may be left off, at first for a short time, then for a few hours, until it is no longer necessary.

Seedling pusillas may be transplanted to individual pots whenever they begin to crowd—or as soon as the minute young leaves show their reddish brown veins.

Early morning sun is all that is necessary to keep pusilla to

ILLUSTRATION 2. Sinningia 'Snowflake' thrives in high humidity. Here, a whole collection grows in a plastic shoebox with a polyethylene cover.

proper symmetry and height. In fact, it seems tolerant of low-light intensity if other conditions are desirable. In a ninth-floor apartment that had only north windows, I had pusilla in flower for months on end in bright daylight, with no sun. I have had equal success with it in an east window with some shading in summer, and also in south and west windows so long as hot, burning sunlight did not reach it for any extended period. And pusilla is a gem for fluorescent light culture. Sometimes it remains in bloom every day for a year or more with such artificial illumination.

﷽ Where To Grow

Pusilla is a fine terrarium plant. Use it as the focal point of a planting in a brandy snifter, or grow one in a tiny crystal goblet or several in a larger container with other tropical plants. Pusillas are especially attractive when planted in neat rows two by two inches apart in a miniature plastic greenhouse. (Instructions for planting terrariums may be found in Chapter 12.)

If a pusilla you have should stop blooming and growing, even under good conditions, allow it go into dormancy for a few weeks by keeping the soil just barely moist and withholding fertilizer. Once new growth is evident, resume regular attentions. Also, do not be alarmed if your plant should be broken off from its small tuber for new growth will appear quickly.

A WORLD OF LITTLE GLOXINIAS

In 1962 when I wrote the first edition of this book, this particular chapter finished with a plea that the plant breeders give us more miniature gloxinias. Well, they have. There has been a population—and popularity—explosion. In fact, some good ones have come and gone, replaced by even better hybrids, in these few years. The following list is suggested by Michael Kartuz; all are unusually well suited to growing under fluorescent lights, all are miniature and all will do well in a terrarium or bottle garden.

'Bright Eyes' is very miniature, slightly larger than *S. pusilla*, with darker purple and larger white-eyed flowers. Delicately veined leaves. Everblooming.

'Cindy' is an outstanding miniature with large slipper-shaped flowers. The top petals are purple, the bottom ones white, with a striped throat. Very free flowering.

'Cindy-Ella' is a tetrapolid version of 'Cindy.' It has slightly larger flowers.

Sinningia concinna closely resembles *S. pusilla* in size, appearance and growing habit. The flowers are much larger

ILLUSTRATION 3. Sinningia concinna *and its offspring: foreground,* S. concinna *in a 2-inch pot; largest plant,* 'Cindy' *and smaller one to the right,* 'Freckles.'

and interestingly marked, shaded purple on white background, with purple-spotted throat.

'Coral Baby' is the best pink-flowered miniature sinningia thus far. The dark coral salmon flowers are produced reliably and plentifully.

'Doll Baby' has large lavender-blue slipper-shaped blooms with yellow throat. It is compact, free-flowering and easy to grow.

'Diploid Doll Baby' is daintier in appearance than 'Doll Baby' with less brittle stems. It also produces more flowers.

'Freckles' has tiny olive-green leaves and an abundance of flowers, the top petals purple, the lower petals white, with a spotted throat.

'Hircon' is a tetrapolid version of 'Freckles,' with fewer but larger flowers.

'Minarette' has large bright pink slipper-shaped flowers. These have warmer pink coloring than the earlier 'Pink Imp,' which this variety has now replaced in the trade.

'Mod Imp' has coral-salmon tubular-shaped flowers and it is considered an improved form of the earlier cultivated 'Modesta.'

'Norma Jean' has rosy orchid, slipper-shaped flowers which it produces freely. Although somewhat variable in color, it is considered a definite improvement, and therefore replacement for the earlier 'Cupid's Doll.'

'Patty Ann' has salmon to salmon-rose, tubular-shaped flowers above plain green, fuzzy leaves almost exactly like

ILLUSTRATION 4. *Closeup of* Sinningia concinna. *(Scale: 2-inch pot.)*

ILLUSTRATION 5.
Sinningia 'Patty
Ann.' (Scale:
2-inch pot.)

some of the old-fashioned florist gloxinias—'Emperor Frederick,' for example.

'Poupee' has lavender-blue, slipper-shaped flowers almost as large as 'Doll Baby,' on a much smaller, more compact plant. It is very free flowering.

'Snowflake' is similar to 'White Sprite,' but with extra petal lobes that give the flowers a fringed effect.

'Tinkerbells' has small olive-green leaves with wiry stems bearing the abundance of rosy purple, tubular flowers. This is especially easy for the beginner.

'White Sprite' is a pure white sport of S. pusilla and it is very free with the flowers.

🌿 OTHER MINIATURE GESNERIADS

Besides the little sinningias, consider miniature African violets (Chapter 3), and in Chapter 11, look up these related plants: *Achimenes, Codonanthe, Columnea, Conandron, Diastema, Episcia, Gesneria, Haberlea, Jankaea, Koellikeria, Kohleria, Nematanthus, Oreocharis, Petrocosmea, Ramonda* and *Streptocarpus.*

ILLUSTRATION 6.
Sinningia 'Snow-
flake.' (Scale:
2-inch pot.)

3. Miniature African Violets

Unless you live in a cave, I am sure you can find a place in your home to grow miniature African violets and so have plants in flower throughout the year. And I should add to this incredible but true statement, that a cave dweller with electricity and fluorescent lights for miniature African violets could beat a window-sill gardener by twice as many blue ribbons. And what space savers are these miniatures. For example, if you have only one window with suitable conditions, it will accommodate four times as many miniatures as it will standard varieties.

Miniature African violets are small scale replicas of the tropical plant known botanically as *Saintpaulia*, a member of the gesneriad family. Saintpaulias are related to *Sinningia pusilla*, other gloxinias, episcias, achimenes and a host of other outstanding indoor plants.

The miniature African violets of today are a far cry from those of ten or twelve years ago. Today's miniatures run the same gamut of color that the standard African violets do. The flowers range up to the size of a quarter and anywhere from six to twenty blossoms is common. The "girl" leaves do not bunch, but lie flat and the plants do not sucker as much. Leaves come tailored, "girl," with raised markings not unlike the fruit of the strawberry, watermelon-striped, quilted, heart-shaped and variegated.

These miniatures are not standard plants that have been kept small through root pruning and cramping in tiny pots nor are they dwarfs. They are true miniatures and will reproduce through leaf cuttings, seeds or suckers.

When you acquire one of these, whether from a grower or your best friend, isolate it for a period of four to six weeks to be sure the plant is healthy. By practicing this preventive quarantine, plus using pasteurized pots, utensils and growing medium, you will be assured the best possible basics for successful growing.

🐜 Pots and Soils

Plastic pots are preferable for these tiny saintpaulias since the soil does not dry out as quickly as it does in clay. The plastic is also easier to keep clean. Pots can be soaked in water and household bleach for a day or so to dissolve the fertilizer salts that have collected on the rim, and then be put through the dishwasher on the hot cycle.

Any light-sterilized or pasteurized soil that is porous, spongy and humusy is good. There are a number of good ones on the market, such as Swiss Farms, New Era Formula Five and Stim-U-Plant—in fact, any soil marked "sterilized African violet soil," is excellent for the miniatures. The addition of super coarse perlite or horticultural vermiculite to these soils will produce a light mix. A ratio of 2-1-1 or 1-1-1 with a handful of charcoal, works well. The soilless mixes such as the Cornell mix or the UCLA mix are also good. The latter two work exceptionally well with wick watering. The mixture should retain moisture, but be airy enough to breathe and open enough to let excess water drain right through.

These little plants should be fed with every watering, using one-fourth the recommended strength of fertilizer. This will

ILLUSTRATION 7. *Collection of miniature African violets, or how to have sixteen different flowering saintpaulias without crowding in a window measuring less than 12 by 24 inches.*

never burn roots even if the plants are dry. African violet foods such as Stim-U-Plant, Peters, Hyponex and Black Magic are all good. It is preferable to alternate two or three different fertilizers and to use plain water, every third or fourth watering, to flush out any collected fertilizer salts. These little plants should never be allowed to become excessively dry as this will encourage sucker growth.

Miniatures do well with wick watering which is a boon to the busy person. Although some varieties have a tendency to grow slightly larger on wicks, unless you intend to show them, the small increase in diameter should not bother you.

A very fine wick is suggested. Fancy glass dishes or baby food jars can be used for the reservoir. If the pot does not fit properly into the opening, a plastic lid, with a hole for the wick, can be used and cut to fit the size of the opening of the container, and hold up the plant. Some wicks do better with a frayed end. Make sure the wick extends well into the pot on one end and to the bottom of the reservoir on the other. Water the plant and wet the wick well before inserting into the container. The same feeding and flushing out schedule as used in regular watering can be used.

Miniatures should be kept in 2½-inch or smaller pots. They can be started in the smaller sizes, 1¼-inch or 2-inch pots, but outside of tiny-leaved plants such as 'Edith's Toy' or 'Allen's Toy,' 2½-inch pots will produce optimum growth and performance. However, owing to horizontally inclined growth, the new miniature semitrailing African violets can be put into a 3-inch squatty pot when they start to look top heavy.

Keep semiminiature plants in pots no larger than a 3-inch squatty. Miniatures and semiminiatures, like the standard African violets, are flat-growing, rosette-forming plants and they look out of proportion in larger or taller pots. Miniatures should never exceed 6 inches in diameter, semiminiatures 8 inches.

Repot miniatures and semiminiatures every three to four months. Remove a row or two of bottom leaves, prune roots slightly, scrape the necks, then put back into the same-sized pot using some fresh soil. The plant growth is from the center, and the lower rows of leaves, as they age, will not produce the bloom again. Any suckers removed at this time can be slanted for propagation the same as leaves. Do not disbud miniatures. When so treated they have been known to go without flowers for a year or more.

🌸 Lights for Little Violets

In winter the miniature African violets do well in east, west or south windows. A thin curtain, tissue or cardboard will protect them at night from a severe temperature drop. In summer months, at times of strong sunlight, they need protection. Unless windows are shaded by trees or shrubbery, they will need a sheet curtain—or transfer them to a north window. The filtered green plastic, used to shade car windshields, can also be used to cover the window pane. It keeps out the hot rays but lets in enough light for good growth.

If grown on a window sill, African violets need a quarter turn every day or two. If they are not turned, one side will lean towards the sun and eventually produce a plant that is leggy or "necky," as the pros say.

Miniatures need the same temperature range as standard African violets—not below 62 degrees at night with a 10-degree rise in the daytime, preferably 75 to 80 degrees. The higher the temperature the more humidity will be necessary. Low temperatures and high humidity will cause mildew. A light spray of Lysol, high above the plants, just letting the mist settle, will keep the plants free of mildew during the times of the year it threatens.

Wherever you live, I am sure you have some place in your home that could be made more interesting by the addition of a fluorescent light unit for growing plants. The miniatures and semiminiatures grow well in lighted carts or homemade stands, with a unit of two 40-watt tubes, in a reflector 13 to 15 inches wide over a shelf or other surface about 2 by 4 feet.

When grown under lights, I find that the miniatures do best

placed 6 to 10 inches below from the edge of the pot to the tubes. Keep the lights on 12 to 16 hours out of every 24, depending on light intensity reflected by surroundings such as white walls. The plants need a period of darkness and too much light will result in damaged foliage—brittle and yellowed—and with the young center leaves distorted with bunchy growth similar to that caused by cyclamen mites. Too little light will cause lack of bloom. Proper light intensity helps set the buds.

A Moist Atmosphere Helps

The best possible method to obtain humidity is to place the plants on trays that are covered with ¼- or ½-inch hardware cloth. The water collects in the bottom of the tray, giving off humidity, and this arrangement is a safety factor to prevent any spread of disease that might occur by using a wet medium such as vermiculite in a community tray. The next best method is to have the pot of each plant resting on pebbles, in its own saucer or dish. The water level in the saucer should never touch the bottom of the pot. Misting or covering the stand with plastic at night are other good ways of increasing the humidity which is needed for good bloom. You can also use a cool-vapor humidifier, either room- or dwelling-sized, to obtain a pleasantly moist atmosphere for your plant—and you.

African Violet Propagation

Miniature African violets are propagated the same as the standards. If you wish to propagate from a leaf, do not use the young center leaves or the old ones at the outer edge, but only the half-matured in a second or third row to produce the best results. Cut the stems no longer than ½ to 1 inch. Insert the leaf stems the full length into moist vermiculite or a combination of vermiculite and perlite with a good handful of charcoal mixed in. Suckers will readily root in the same mixture and rapidly produce little plants. Watering with a good fungicide will keep the leaves from damping off.

When large enough to handle, pot up individually in small pots or in community trays such as plastic bread boxes, shoe boxes or aluminum pans. Punch out drainage holes. Keep the medium moist at all times. Unless your growing area has good humidity, cover the leaves with the top of the plastic box, keeping the corner of the lid raised a little, or insert the aluminum pan in a plastic bag. Give them good light but not hot, hot sun.

Allow the plantlets to reach at least an inch in height, with four true leaves, before separating them from the parent leaf. Separate them carefully with as much of the rooting material as you can and as little damage as possible. The plantlets can then be potted up separately or again put into a community pan until the pan is crowded. Keep the humidity high and don't let them get excessively dry for the next seven to ten days.

Besides the usefulness of miniatures in conventional pots, they are delightful for open terrariums with open woodland landscapes or as jewel-like focal points for plantings in such crystal containers as goblets, brandy snifters, globes and candy or apothecary jars.

❧ FAVORITE LITTLE AFRICAN VIOLETS

'Bergen Strawberry Sherbet'—Semidouble pink, white and green bloom over quilted foliage. Semiminiature.

'Calico Kitten'—Round leaves, variegated cream, pink and green. Many double blue blossoms. Miniature.

'Cheer U'—Double white with a blue edge. Serrated tailored foliage. Semiminiature.

'Coco'—Double white with a blue eye. Blooms have a lacy edge and the leaves are tiny and tailored. Miniature.

'Coral Satin'—Single coral pink on oval quilted foliage. Semiminiature.

ILLUSTRATION 8. *'Pixie Blue'*
miniature African violet.
(Scale: 2-inch pot.)

'Dancing Doll'—Double bright pink star on ovate foliage. Blooms profusely. Semiminiature.

'Double Take'—Double pansy-purple star with quilted oval leaves.

'Icicle Trinket'—Huge double white blooms on variegated, serrated foliage. The variegation is around the edges of each leaf. Semiminiature.

'Loverly'—Semidouble mauve, plum geneva with variegated foliage. Semiminiature.

'Lucky Locket'—Semidouble white star, sometimes pink-striped with fern green, tailored leaves. Miniature.

'Midget Bon Bon'—Single round pink flower on beautiful variegated tailored leaves. Forms a perfect rosette. Stays small. Miniature.

'Mini-Mignon'—Double amethyst star with tailored leaves. Forms a perfect rosette and holds the bloom high, evenly centered around the plant.

'Naughty N'Nice'—Double dark fuchsia star with some white on quilted round foliage. Semiminiature.

'Pique Pixie'—Single pink. Miniature semitrailer. Covers itself with bloom.

'Silver Bells'—Single white bell with tiny glossy foliage. Miniature.

'Small Change'—Double royal purple star in quilted oval foliage. Huge flowers. Miniature.

ILLUSTRATION 9. *'Tiny Ellie' miniature African violet growing in a shell.*

ILLUSTRATION 10. *'Violet Trail' miniature African violet; note distinctive star-shaped flowers. (Scale: 2-inch pot.)*

ILLUSTRATION 11. *'Silver Bells' miniature African violet has white flowers that seem to be more Canterbury bell than African violet. (Scale: 2-inch pot.)*

ILLUSTRATION 12: *'Pink Trail' miniature African violet. (Scale: 2-inch pot.)*

'Tiny Ellie'—Double rose-pink star on dark tailored foliage. A profuse bloomer. The combination of roys pink and the dark foliage is beautiful.

'Tiny Pink Bells'—Little hanging pink bells. Profuse bloomer.

'Tiny Sparkles'—Double burgundy, tipped with white dots on dark foliage. Flowers cover the foliage and it looks like a nosegay.

'Tippy Pink'—Single pink with a white tip. Tailored round foliage. Miniature.

4. Miniature Begonias

Plant breeders could and should have a field day creating true miniature begonias. There are already some small ones—more than sixty varieties described in literature as miniatures and dwarfs are included in this chapter—but as most of these grow beyond early youth, they attain girth and considerable stature. However, as baby plants they are precocious delights. Start with the smallest specimen you can get, or from seeds if these are available, and enjoy your "miniature" until it outgrows the allotted space. Then, or just before, start a new plant of the same variety so as to have another young sprout coming on.

If there were a medal for the best house plants, I would award it, a shiny gold one, to begonias. They are also year-round troupers for the home greenhouse and for growing under fluorescent lights. The species and varieties illustrated and discussed here thrive through the winter in east, south or west windows, or in a well-ventilated greenhouse that receives partial to full sunlight. (Under fluorescent lights treat them the same as you would treat African violets, described in Chapter 3.) During the summer, hot and direct sun will scorch the leaves (except *possibly* the semperflorens or wax varieties which can be useful outdoors in a sunny spot if in constantly moist, humusy soil). Provide full shade in the greenhouse, and for a window garden supply a curtain unless deciduous trees or shrubs afford shade from outdoors.

☘ How To Grow

Begonias thrive in warmth and humidity. How warm? Comfortable for you, or specifically, a range of 60 to 80 degrees. They need at least 40 per cent humidity, 50 is better, and results should be superb in air that contains as much as 60 to 70 per cent. Most begonias need fresh air, however, so if you plant them in a terrarium, let the covering over the top stay open enough to allow some fresh air to circulate inside.

Begonias thrive in a mixture of equal parts garden soil, leaf mold, sharp sand and peat moss. The addition of one part well-rotted cow manure will improve growth. Begonias also do well in the Michael Kartuz G-B-S Mix (described in Chapter 2) or in almost any soil that will grow healthy and flowering African violets. A dilute feeding of liquid house-plant fertilizer, applied every three or four weeks when plants are growing, will benefit them.

Begonia roots should be kept nicely moist at all times. The varieties with succulent, fleshy rhizomes (classified as rhizomatous) can generally stand more dryness than the others. After you water a begonia, it will not suffer if the base of the pot rests in water for an hour or two, but don't let water stand all day or overnight.

☘ Propagation

Semperflorens or wax begonias are easy to grow from their dust-fine seeds. These may be sown in warmth and moistness at any time of the year, but they germinate best in late winter or spring. Other begonias also grow easily from seeds, though most of the hybrids do not come true, and none of the rex varieties do.

The propagation of begonias by leaf and stem cuttings is easy and rewarding. The rhizomes of rhizomatous varieties and the rex types may be cut into small pieces, each containing at least one leaf bud, and rooted in a moist mixture of sand and peat moss or G-B-S Mix (Chapter 2) in high humidity.

Rhizomatous begonias send their trailing stems along the ground, eventually swooping over the edge of the pot. Such begonias can be divided at any time, but preferably in the spring after they stop blooming. Shake off the old soil, gently pry and cut apart the roots and rhizomes. Remove the old leaves, leaving just the fresh young ones. Repot in moist soil and place in a moist atmosphere in moderate warmth and well-circulated air.

🌿 FAVORITE MINIATURE AND SMALL BEGONIAS

In these descriptions, I have indicated uses for each plant, that is whether for pot culture, a hanging basket or terrarium culture. (Information about designing and planting terrarium gardens may be found in Chapter 12.)

'Andy' a semperflorens, grows 4 to 6 inches tall, and forms a neat plant of succulent, bright grass-green leaves. It bears single flowers of glowing rose-pink. Propagate by seeds or cuttings. For pots.

'Baby Perfectifolia' is a rhizomatous miniature with small pink flowers in winter and spring. It is a fairly new variety, similar in size to 'China Doll.' For pots, baskets and terrariums.

ILLUSTRATION 13. Begonia aridicaulis. *(Scale: 3-inch pot.)*

ILLUSTRATION 14. Begonia rex *'Baby Rainbow.'* *(Scale: 2-inch pot.)*

'Baby Rainbow' is a rex miniature with puckered leaves of rich, iridescent rainbow colors. For small pots, or outstanding in a terrarium.

'Beatrice Haddrell' is a rhizomatous miniature with a star-like leaf of very dark, purple-black and irregular green veins. It has pink flowers in winter and spring. For pots, baskets and terrariums.

'Bowerae' (Illustration 16) is a rhizomatous, known popularly as the eyelash begonia because of the fetching white hairs spaced evenly around the edges of the chartreuse leaves, the margins of which are spotted with purple-brown areas. The flowers of palest pink appear over a long period, particularly in winter and spring. For pots, baskets and terrariums.

ILLUSTRATION 15. Begonia rex *'Bantam Gem.'* *(Scale: 2-inch pot.)*

'Bow-Arriola' (Illustration 17) is rhizomatous, one of the many hybrids of 'Bowerae.' The edges of the dark green, chocolate-marked leaves are eyelashed with white hairs, and the winter and spring flowers of medium pink are showy. For pots or baskets.

'Bow-Joe' (Illustration 18) is rhizomatous with reddish, black-brown leaves, and a chartreuse star at the sinus. The pink flowers appear profusely in winter and spring, even on plants 8 inches tall in 2¼-inch pots. The backs of the petals are dotted with vivid, warm red. For pots, baskets and terrariums.

'Chantilly Lace' (Illustration 19) is rhizomatous with a small-lobed, chartreuse, cupped leaf, up to 3 inches in length, with dark black stitching and eyelash hairs along the edges. It has clusters of pale pink flowers in the winter and spring. For pots, baskets or terrariums.

'China Doll' is a delightful miniature. It is rhizomatous with leaves of light green to almost solid purple-black, wide brown veins, and hairs along the leaf edges and stems that glisten in the sunlight. It has tiny, pink flowers in winter and spring. For pots, baskets and terrariums.

'Foliosa,' the fern-leaf begonia, is probably the smallest-leaved of all begonias. The reddish-brown, much-branched stems are set with opposite, notched leaves of dark bronze-green. The small white flowers are borne at the ends of the arching, drooping branches. This is a choice miniature if started from a 2- to 3-inch rooted cutting, and then kept clipped and trained to desired size. For pots, baskets or terrariums.

ILLUSTRATION 16. Begonia bowerae.

ILLUSTRATION 17. Begonia
'Bow-Arriola.'

ILLUSTRATION 18. Begonia
'Bow-Joe.'

ILLUSTRATION 19. Begonia
'Chantilly Lace.'

ILLUSTRATION 20. Begonia hydrocotylifolia.

B. hydrocotylifolia (Illustration 20), the pennywort or miniature pond-lily begonia, is a small-growing rhizomatous type, similar in appearance to the old-fashioned beefsteak begonia. It has bright pink flowers in winter and spring, with round, dark green leaves tinted a darker, brown-green along the veins. For pots, baskets or terrariums.

'It' is a rex with green leaves heavily brushed with silver. The flowers of bright, vibrant pink measure up to an inch across and are borne well above the foliage. They appear even in midwinter and on into spring. For pots or terrariums.

'Lorraine Closson,' 'Louise Closson,' 'Lucille Closson' and 'Lucy Closson' are all classified as miniature rexes with dark, metallic leaves combined in various ways with suffusions and markings of richest purple, pink, lavender and red. A delightful quartet for pots and terrariums.

'Maphil' is rhizomatous with chartreuse leaves dashingly marked with reddish, chocolate-brown. It sends up clusters of pink flowers in the winter and spring; foliage outstanding all year. For pots, baskets or terrariums.

ILLUSTRATION 21. Begonia rex *'Wood Nymph.'* *(Scale: 2-inch pot.)*

ILLUSTRATION 22. Begonia bowerae nigra-marga. *(Scale: 3-inch pot.)*

ILLUSTRATION 23. Begonia *'Cathedral.'* *(Scale: 3-inch pot.)*

'Pied Piper' is a dwarf semperflorens with pink, double flowers, the centers crested into the shape of a thimble. For pots or baskets.

'Pistachio' is a very dwarf semperflorens begonia with flowers that open with a center crest of light green, but as they age, this changes to yellow, set off by outer petals of pink. For pots or baskets.

'Red Berry' is a miniature rex suffused with intense maroon red all over. For pots or terrariums.

'Richard Robinson' is a small-growing fibrous-rooted variety with maple-like leaves of light green, almost entirely covered with metallic silver. A beautiful plant, particularly choice for a terrarium.

B. rotundifolia is a Haitian miniature with round leaves of light green, contrasting with red petioles. It sends forth white flowers over a long season. For pots and terrariums.

'Spaulding' is a rhizomatous begonia introduced as a miniature, but a variety that may quickly exceed 12 inches in diameter. However, it will bloom profusely even in a thumb pot while young, the flowers reaching to 10 inches, the foliage a span of 5 inches. The flowers are pink, and the young leaves are chartreuse with bold veins of red-brown. As they mature the vein coloring blends into the leaf. For pots or hanging baskets; terrariums while young.

ILLUSTRATION 24. Begonia conchifolia. *(Scale: 2-inch pot.)*

ILLUSTRATION 25.
Begonia herbacea.
(Scale: 2-inch pot.)

ILLUSTRATION 26. Begonia prismatocarpa. *(Scale: 2-inch pots.)*

ILLUSTRATION 27.
*Begonia 'Dres-
den Gold.'*
*(Scale: leaf 2
inches long.)*

In addition to these old favorite small-growing begonias, I am now growing many others that have been more recently introduced and are recommended by friends who specialize in begonias. First, the list of Joy Logee Martin of Logee's Greenhouses, Danielson, Connecticut:

REXES:	'Bantam Gem'
	'Frosty'
	'Granny'
	'Peridot' ("tiniest")
	'Shirt Sleeve'
	'Wood Nymph'
RHIZOMATOUS:	*B. aridicaulis*
	B. 'Bowerae' *nigra-marga*
	'Cathedral'
	'Chimborazo'
	B. conchifolia
	'Gaystar'
	B. herbacea
	'Nora Bedson'
	B. polygonoides
	B. prismatocarpa
	'Red Planet'
	'Red Spider'
	B. schmidtiana
	'Sun Gold'

My second listing of miniature begonias comes from Mary Ellen Ross of Merry Gardens, Camden, Maine, who suggests many from Mrs. Martin's and my lists, plus these rhizomatous types: 'Aquarius,' 'Aries,' 'Blinkum,' 'Universe,' 'Winkum' and 'Zip.'

Michael Kartuz of 92 Chestnut Street, Wilmington, Massachusetts, adds to all of our lists with these suggestions:

TRAILING: *B. maxwelton*

REXES: 'Dew Drop'
                 'Northern Lights'
                 'Our Indian'
                 'Peacock'
                 'Red Mystery'
                 'Robin'
                 'Thrush'

RHIZOMATOUS: 'Black Watch'
                 B. brooksii
                 B. conchifolia
                 'Little Darling'
                 B. metachroa
                 'Midget'
                 'Ministar'
                 B. nurii
                 'Plejeba'
                 'Robert Shatzer'
                 'Smidgens'
                 'Squiggles'
                 'Starbaby'
                 B. subnummularifolia
                 'Tracery'

5. Miniature Daffodils and Other Little Bulbs for Forcing

Golden daffodils 3 inches tall with rushlike foliage; purple tulips but 4 inches overall; small sunny crocuses in the middle of winter; miniature hyacinths in bloom for New Year's Eve —these are some of the little bulbous plants that can be forced into bloom on a sunny, moderate-to-cool window sill, in a home greenhouse or under fluorescent lights in a cool room or basement.

These bulbs are forced in the same way as the large ones. Since they are small, it is possible to plant up to six of one variety in a 4- or 5-inch pot, or to put just one in a 2¼-inch container; or three to a 3-inch pot. A satisfactory potting soil consists of equal parts garden loam, sand (or perlite) and peat moss.

🌺 How To Force

Miniature bulbs for forcing should be ordered in the summer and potted immediately upon receipt, usually in late September or early October, with the tops of the bulbs just beneath the surface of the soil. Water well and place in a cold frame or in some dark place where the temperature will be between 40 and 50 degrees F. Keep the soil moist, and be sure temperatures do not rise above 50 degrees for any length of time, or go below zero. In a cold frame, put a layer of clean sand over the pots and then cover with a mulch of straw or peat moss. The layer of sand makes it easier to lift the pots out of the frame, and bring them out cleaner than they would be with peat moss piled directly on top. Or you can keep them clean by covering each pot with an inverted pot of the same size. I have also had good results in covering the pots with 4 to 8 inches of sand and no other covering.

After rooting, as you begin forcing, keep in mind that blooms will be of better quality, though not so fast to mature, if plants are forced slowly in temperatures not above 60 degrees F. Although drying out at the time roots are forming may be harmful, it is certainly disastrous after leaves push up, and flower buds swell. Furthermore, dryness in the air and excessive heat will cause blasted buds and premature yellowing of foliage.

As soon as leaves and buds begin active growth, apply biweekly feedings of one-half- to one-third-strength fertilizer, continuing the feeding throughout the growing season. After these little bulbs are forced in my sunny, cool window garden and in the greenhouse, I continue to take good care of them. When the weather warms so that succulent, forced foliage will not be harmed by a cold snap, I sink the pots outdoors in a warm, sunny cold frame, and continue regular watering until foliage ripens and turns yellow of its own accord.

Pots are left in the frame without particular attention until cold weather. Bulbs are then repotted, returned to the cold frame, covered with sand and peat and remain there until early January, when they are brought indoors in weekly succession and forced as usual. Second-year results are not always as excellent as first-year, but I have been pleased with the way a number of the bulbs have multiplied and thrived under continuous pot culture.

Trouble-free Way to Force Bulbs

Last fall I moved to a new house too late in the season for me to build a cold frame, or do any outdoor gardening. I had miniature bulbs on order (it's an annual affair—a note on my calendar in July to order plenty of miniature bulbs for winter and spring forcing), so when they came I potted them as usual, moistened the soil, and then set the pots in flats of moist peat moss and sand on the floor of the garage—unheated, but attached to the house. Temperatures there frequently went below freezing but stayed generally in the range of 40 to 55 degrees F. I watered the bulbs as often as necessary, about twice a month, and, from early February on, every pot forced well and yielded perfect bloom—certainly an easy, trouble-free way to force bulbs.

A DOZEN GOOD MINIATURE DAFFODILS (NARCISSUS)

N. asturiensis (minimus), 3 to 6 inches, has a tiny yellow trumpet, perfectly formed and not much over an inch long. (See Illustration 28.)

N. bulbocodium conspicuous, 6 inches, is the yellow hoop-petticoat daffodil with flowers of a rich golden color, 1¼-inches long with a wide mouth an inch across. Foliage is rushlike.

N. bulbocodium obesus (Illustration 28), 3 to 5 inches, has small, creeping leaves, and hoop-petticoat flowers of bright, clear yellow.

N. campernelli 'Orange Queen,' 10 inches, has fragrant flowers of apricot-orange, clustered four on a stem. It performs perfectly when forced.

N. canaliculatus, 6 inches, has narrow, erect, blue-green leaves. It bears heads of three or four sweet-scented flowers with a white perianth and globular golden cup.

N. cyclamineus, 6 inches, has a downward painted trumpet of vibrant yellow, a half inch wide and frilled at the edge. The perianth reflexes sharply.

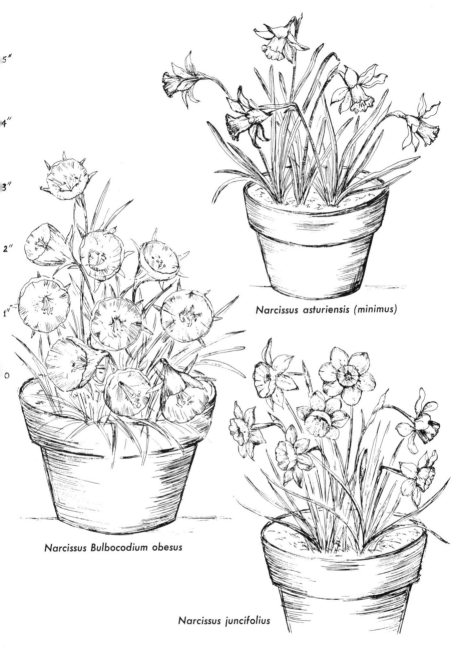

5"

4"

3"

2"

1"

0

Narcissus asturiensis (minimus)

Narcissus Bulbocodium obesus

Narcissus juncifolius

ILLUSTRATION 28. *Three favorite little daffodils.*

N. juncifolius (Illustration 28), 3 to 5 inches, has small, graceful flowers of rich yellow with a dainty, flat crown.

'March Sunshine,' 9 inches, is another variety of *cyclamineus*, valuable for forcing. It has a slender tubelike cup of yellow, and starry, slightly reflexed petals of yellow.

N. nanus, 3 inches, is the smallest trumpet daffodil; the flowers are bright, buttercup yellow. It is excellent for forcing.

N. obvallaris, 9 inches, the Tenby daffodil, is an early variety, especially valued for forcing. It bears medium-sized flowers of sunny, intense yellow on sturdy stems.

N. triandrus albus, 7 inches, angel's tears daffodil, has clusters of cream-white flowers with perianth reflexed sharply, and a globular cup that points down. This is one of the most charming of all miniature daffodils.

N. watieri, 4 inches, has flat, tiny flowers of pure white. This species is without peer for miniature gardens.

'W. P. Milner,' 12 inches, is a miniature trumpet daffodil with small, sulfur-white, nodding flowers, and the fragrance of a cowslip. It is one of the best small daffodils for forcing.

ILLUSTRATION 29. Narcissus jonquilla simplex—*exquisite perfection in a miniature. (Scale: 5-inch pot.)*

🌿 NINE DELIGHTFUL MINIATURE TULIPS (TULIPA)

T. batalinii 'Bright Gem,' 5 inches, has cup-shaped sulfur-yellow flowers tinted apricot-pink.

'Berlioz,' 5 inches, a *kaufmanniana* variety, has flowers of citron-yellow, the outside petals tinted red. Foliage is patterned with brown.

T. cretica, 4 inches, has a flower that is almost white, but lightly blushed with pink, and a yellow spot at the base.

'Gaiety,' 4 inches, a *kaufmanniana* variety, has very large flowers similar to a water-lily, cream-white on the inside, with a bold center of apricot-orange, flushed outside with rose-pink.

T. persica, 5 inches, sometimes known as *brevniana,* is a late cluster- or bunch-flowering tulip. The starry blooms are bright yellow inside, flushed with apricot or bronze.

T. pulchella humilis, 4 inches, has lavender-pink, globe-shaped flowers. Var. 'Violet Queen,' 4 inches, has cup-shaped

ILLUSTRATION 30. *Miniature daffodil hybrid 'W. P. Milner.' (Scale: 5-inch pot.)*

ILLUSTRATION 31. *Eranthis, the winter-aconite. Photograph courtesy the Netherlands Flower-Bulb Institute.*

flowers of rich purple-red. Both of these bloom outdoors in earliest spring—sometimes in February—and for us they have given a good account of themselves when forced in a cool place in early February.

'Robert Stolz,' 5 inches, a *kaufmanniana*, has scarlet flowers, the throat yellow and black. Leaves are variegated with purple.

T. tarda, 3 inches, sends up several starry flowers at one time, the outer petals tinted green, and the throat of the bloom a pale yellow that fades to white toward the petal tips.

T. urumiensis, 6 inches, has a rosette of leaves and large sunny yellow flowers. Outer petals are tinted apricot or bronze.

🍂 OTHER SMALL BULBS FOR FORCING

Brodiaea, calochortus, chionodoxa, winter-flowering crocus (varieties of *C. biflorus, chrysanthus, sieberi, tomasinianus* and *vernus* in particular), eranthis (winter aconite) erythronium, *Hyacinthus amethystinus albus,* and *coerulea,* also *H. azureus* and *H. dalmaticus,* muscari (grape-hyacinths), puschkinia, and galanthus (snowdrops) are delightful to force in small pots for mid- to late-winter bloom in a cool window or greenhouse.

Two miniature varieties of the regular showy or exhibition hyacinths are now offered. They are larger than most of the bulbs included here, but still rate as small growers. 'Rosalie' sends up dainty stems of fragrant, pink flowers; 'Vanguard' is light blue. Both may be forced to bloom for Christmas, and will continue for several weeks as new flower sprays develop.

All these small bulbs are listed in the fall catalogs of bulb specialists. Make your selections from among those small varieties or species that naturally flower earliest. Chances are they will be the best for forcing.

6. Miniature Evergreens

Tiny, perfectly-formed evergreens, less than 6 inches tall at ten years of age, are replicas of hardy types cultivated in gardens all over the country. Some slow-growing evergreens are natural miniatures; others are dwarfed by the rootstock onto which they are grafted; and still others are man-made dwarfs created by bonsai culture. It is the natural miniatures that I will discuss here for these are well suited to culture in pots or for the miniature gardens described in Chapter 12.

True miniature evergreens usually originate from seeds, or by mutations or sports that are propagated by cuttings. They are beautiful for their shape, coloring, and texture, yet they are easily maintained. In the course of a year most of them grow no more than an inch wider or an inch taller. They remain as bright in midwinter as in summer, and some like *Thuja orientalis juniperioides* take on a different color in the cool seasons.

Miniature conifers do well in semishade to full sun in a cool room or greenhouse—preferably with a maximum of 60 degrees F. in the winter, although higher temperatures are not harmful if air and soil are moist. Foliage benefits from frequent syringing. When this is done, care should be taken that moisture on the foliage does not collect to the point of draining into the soil and making it water-logged, unless it is dry enough to need water anyway. A suitable growing medium consists of equal parts garden loam, sand, peat moss and rich leaf mold or compost.

The names of miniature evergreens are long and complicated. What's more, they are badly confused. In these descriptions I have listed only available varieties, and by the names under which they are sold. Illustration 32 indicates the basic forms—columnar or spire-shaped, conical, pyramidal, funnel-shaped, globular or spherical, and pendulous.

☙ THIRTY ATTRACTIVE MINIATURE EVERGREENS

Abies balsamea nana (fir) is a slow-growing, very small globe-shaped evergreen.

Chamaecyparis (cypress) *lawsoniana forsteckiensis*, a dense-needled tree, round and fat except for the tapering central leader that grows up to a point.

C. lawsoniana minima aurea forms a compact, rounded bush of rich, golden branchlets.

C. lawsoniana minima glauca grows very slowly as a glaucous ball or broad cone of blue.

C. obtusa coralliformis is a most unusual miniature with coral-red branchlets.

ILLUSTRATION 32. *Basic shapes of miniature evergreens.*

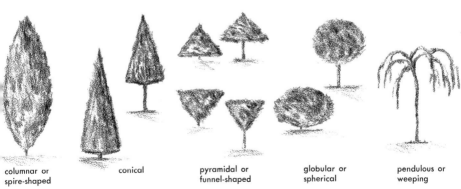

| columnar or spire-shaped | conical | pyramidal or funnel-shaped | globular or spherical | pendulous or weeping |

ILLUSTRATION 33. Juniperus communis compressa. ILLUSTRATION 34. Picea excelsa clanbrasiliana.

C. obtusa juniperiodes is one of the slowest growing and best choices for a miniature garden; it makes a minute ball of fan-shaped branchlets.

C. obtusa lycopoides aurea has fine-textured golden foliage on short, twisted branchlets.

C. obtusa nana aurea grows as a globe of golden, fan-shaped branchlets densely set with needles.

C. pisifera filifera nana is a miniature with blue-green leaves densely set on the branchlets; var. *variegata* has the same growth, but needles are yellow tipped.

C. pisifera plumosa cyanea viridis forms a compact, very beautiful globe of blue-gray.

C. pisifera plumosa juniperioides is of dense, compact co-lumnar habit, the branchlets set with golden-green needles.

C. pisifera squamata intermedia is a miniature of irregular shape, but always dense and slow growing with light green foliage.

C. pisifera squamata pygmaea grows as a dense, miniature shrublet with soft glaucous foliage.

Cryptomeria Bandai-Sugi forms an irregular mound of green.

C. pygmaea nana grows very slowly in pendulous habit; a handsome little tree.

C. vilmoriniana grows as a globe, and is one of the best miniatures for a garden in a trough, or large, shallow pot.

Juniperus (juniper) *chinensis albo-variegata* forms a compact, prostrate-to-small, blue-green pyramid with the needles white tipped.

J. chinensis Blaauw's variety, one of the best slow-growing shrublets, is covered with green-blue needles.

J. communis compressa (Illustration 33) is a miniature Irish juniper with a slender columnar shape, very slow growing, and one of the best for a miniature garden.

J. communis prostrata is trailing or pendulous with brilliant glaucous foliage.

J. procumbens nana is a creeping or pendulous miniature with dense, dark green foliage; var. *glauca* has blue needles.

J. scopulorum horizontalis glauca forms a low pyramid of closely packed branchlets with gray-green needles.

J. squamata Meyeri is of bushy, upright habit with steel-gray needles.

Picea (spruce) *excelsa clanbrasiliana* (Illustration 34) has pine-scented branchlets, bright green at first, maturing darker. It grows as a small bush, sometimes of near funnel shape.

P. excelsa pumila is a dense, low-growing shrublet with dark green needles and fan-shaped branches; bushy or funnel-shaped.

Taxus (yew) *baccata fastigiata Standishii* has golden needles and a pyramidal shape.

Thuja (arbor-vitae) *globosa* is a mound of green in warm weather; brown in winter.

T. occidentalis ohlendorfi (syn. *spaethii*) makes a round bush of slender, graceful branchlets.

T. occidentalis plicata Rogersii aurea is a very slow-growing pyramid of golden needles; an excellent choice for a miniature garden landscape.

T. orientalis juniperioides has gray needles in summer, turning to plum in winter, on a fine-textured globe shape. It is a beauty.

7. Miniature Geraniums

Miniature geraniums are great in the house or greenhouse. Give them sunshine (an unshaded south, east or west window or a sunny greenhouse), or 14 to 16 hours of fluorescent illumination, and they'll bloom for months on end, never outgrowing 2½- to 4-inch pots. Besides dashing colors of flowers, they have attractive foliage every day of the year. More than seventy-five different varieties appear in catalogs. Even if space for plants in your apartment or house is limited to just *one average-size window* that receives east, south or west sunlight, you can install glass shelves and grow as many as twenty-five different miniature geraniums in it. But then, telling you the wonders of geraniums is like trying to say why we all admire the rose. Whether you grow just one, or all of them, I am certain that these diminutive geraniums will give you much and continued enjoyment per square inch of growing space.

Culture of Little Geraniums

Grow these perky geraniums in a mixture of equal parts sand and good garden soil. The sand aerates the medium and allows the roots to breathe; the soil gives them nourishment. One grower I know uses just garden soil. Another, an apartment dweller, told me he used Black Magic African Violet Mix for miniature geraniums growing under fluorescent lights. I couldn't believe him until I tried it myself, and now I know it works. In fact, I had the nerve to put the reputedly difficult 'Black Vesuvius' in Black Magic and it bloomed for months on end!

Whatever the medium you choose, keep it evenly moist at all times. If this seems like an indefinite statement, then consider it this way: We like chocolate cake that is neither dried out and stale, nor soggy. Just pleasantly moist and crumbly. Miniature geraniums have the same taste for moisture: damp to the touch of your finger, but not powdery and not muddy. Since these geraniums grow in small pots, they need water frequently. Apply it at the rim of the pot, and do not let the base stand in a saucer of water for more than a few minutes. Plants growing in little clay pots require water more often than those in plastic, almost daily compared to every third day.

Miniature geraniums may be started and maintained for years in 2½- or 3-inch pots. The more vigorous semi-dwarfs may be started in thumb pots, but eventually they will need 3- or 4-inch containers. They become pot-bound more quickly than true miniatures and require repotting more frequently. White or pastel green plastic or standard clay pots are all attractive for geraniums. More important than color is their need for a drainage hole.

Geraniums thrive in temperatures of 55 to 70 degrees F., with a drop of 10 degrees F. at night.

Most of these geraniums are more compact and bushy if the growing tips are pinched off when the plants are young, and again after a long period of bloom. Pinching delays flowering, so if your plant is reasonably compact, you may prefer to let it alone and enjoy early flowers. After a year in one container, promote vigorous new growth by pruning back the old plant, trimming off old roots that wind around and around the root ball and repotting in fresh soil. Root the trimmings of half-ripened branches to get more plants exactly like the ones from which they were pruned.

🐦 Propagation

Tip cuttings an inch or longer of half-ripened growth (not soft and succulent; not hard and woody) will root quickly in warm, 72 degrees F., moist sand. Or insert each cutting in a small pot in which it will grow, using the standard potting soil. Keep the rooting medium moist at all times. For a few days, place the cutting out of strong sun, preferably in a bright north window where the air is moist but not densely humid. If you root the cuttings in sand alone, then be sure to pot them as soon as roots develop. To check on this, use a pencil or knife to loosen the sand around the cutting. Remove it gently, and if roots show, even one, pot immediately. If there are none, firm the sand back around the cutting and wait a week or two before checking again.

🐦 Promoting Flowers

If your miniature geranium looks healthy but doesn't bloom, chances are it is not receiving enough warmth and sun. If you can't provide more sunshine, then fluorescent light may be the answer. The true miniature varieties grow and flower well all through the year when placed about 4 inches below two or three 40-watt daylight fluorescent tubes that are kept on 14 to 16 hours out of every twenty-four. Avoid fertilizer with a high nitrogen content. It may cause geraniums to develop foliage at the expense of flowers.

A common problem with geraniums of every size is that the lower leaves turn yellow and fall off, eventually leaving bushy growth at the top, a pot at the bottom, and bare stems in between. If you have had this happen, check these possible causes: temperatures that fluctuate widely from very cold to arid heat; humid, stuffy air that does not circulate—usually resulting from growing the plants too close together, or in a closed container such as a terrarium, or in a room that has no ventilation; soil that is too dry (water more) or too wet (don't water so much). Occasionally a leak of manufactured gas will cause geranium leaves to turn yellow. If you are sure that your conditions are culturally perfect, then check lines to stove, refrigerator, drier or other appliance using gas. If all of the leaves on a geranium tend to be yellow-green or pale, the plant may be starved for plant food. Begin with dilute feeding (one-half or one-third recommended strength) applied every other week. When foliage is again of healthy color, reduce feedings to every 3 or 4 weeks.

If you notice that your geranium has suddenly begun to wither and appear lifeless, check the stem. It is probably black, most noticeably near the soil, but also to some extent up the stem. This black rot is the result of overwatering a clay soil that packs and prevents moisture from draining off and keeps roots from having enough air. Once a plant gets rot, all you can do is cut off the top part, trim away affected portions, root those that are healthy, and throw away the rest —plant, soil and all.

❧ Grow a Miniature to Tree Form

Just as standard zonale and ivy-leaved geraniums are grown to tree form, so can the miniature and semi-dwarfs. Start with a young, rooted cutting that is straight and unbranched. Turn the pot often, even daily, so that each side of the cutting receives its share of sun. As the plant elongates, allow no new growth tips to develop, but guard the main tip of the stem. If shoots push out along the sides of the one trunk or stem, rub these off with index finger and thumb. When the plant reaches 10, 12, or however many inches tall you want your geranium tree to be, shape and trim the top growth allowing roughly two-thirds to one-half of the total height to remain as bare trunk, the rest a ball of foliage with flowers at the top. Support the trunk with a stake.

Unless you live near a grower of miniature geraniums (listed at the back of the book) you will have to obtain your collection by mail. Some varieties ship well, others resent the necessarily close and damp conditions, and arrive with yellowing foliage, even powdery mildew. As soon as they arrive, unwrap the plants, water them if they are dry, and let them have fresh air (not a cold draft, of course). If the leaves are covered with gray powdery mildew, apply horticultural dusting sulfur.

🪴 FAVORITE MINIATURE GERANIUMS

In this list, I have indicated both miniature and semidwarf plants. I would like to be more specific about heights for each plant. However, because maximum height varies with climate and culture, it is impossible to say exactly. The varieties I have tagged here as miniatures are those that in my experience stay under 6 inches; the semidwarfs are those that exceed 6 inches, probably stay under 10, but sometimes grow to 16 inches. Rich, moist soil will grow larger miniature geraniums, although they are less prone to rank, succulent growth than standard zonales.

'Alcyone' has a typical zonale leaf, not richly marked, but a dark attractive green. Large leaves reach 1½ inches in diameter. Clusters of rose-pink buds open to umbels of six or more bright pink, slender-petaled flowers. A miniature, this will begin to flower at 2 inches.

'Arcturus' begins to bear bright scarlet, double flowers when less than 3 inches tall. They are displayed above heavily frilled leaves that grow on branching stems. A semidwarf.

'Bashful' is a miniature prized for its large, rounded flowers of lavender.

'Black Vesuvius' is one of the smallest miniature geraniums. Its dark green leaves are zoned ripe-olive black, and they form a petite plant that displays umbels of ridiculously large orange-scarlet flowers.

'Brooks Barnes' has dark foliage and large, rounded, salmon-pink single flowers in big clusters on a plant that is miniature

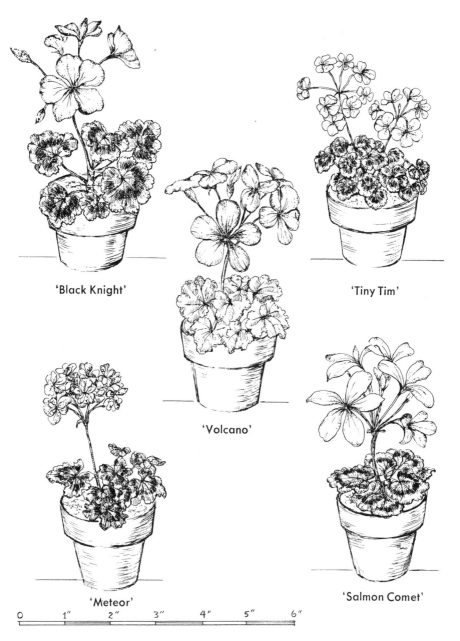

'Black Knight'

'Tiny Tim'

'Volcano'

'Meteor'

'Salmon Comet'

0   1"   2"   3"   4"   5"   6"

ILLUSTRATION 35. *Collection of miniature geraniums.*

and slow-growing. 'Black Knight' (formerly called 'Red Brooks Barnes') has orange-red flowers and is considered an improved form of 'Black Vesuvius.' (See Illustration 35.)

'Brownie' has zonale leaves, golden brown at first, with a distinctive zone. It bears quantities of scarlet, single flowers, branches readily, and grows as a semidwarf.

'Capella' is a vigorous miniature with rich, forest-green zonale foliage and double, salmon-pink flowers of twisted, sometimes quilled petals.

'Doc' displays vivid scarlet flowers on a vigorous, semidwarf plant. The foliage is bright green, and the blooms are abundant.

'Dopey' is one of the best of the semidwarfs. It has umbels of pink to rose-red flowers, each with a distinctive white eye. 'Dopey' is a robust grower and a good choice for less than perfect conditions.

'Emma Hossler' begins to produce its light pink, white-eyed, double flowers when it is just 3 or 4 inches tall, but ultimately it may grow to 12 inches or more in height, and is classed as a semidwarf. It forms a compact, branched plant with attractive rounded zonale leaves and a profusion of flowers.

'Epsilon' is a semidwarf with rounded, full flowers of petal pink, each enhanced by a bright eye of shocking pink. These appear above lively, grass-green foliage.

'Fairy Tales' is a miniature with dark-zoned leaves and large, ruffled, single flowers of white, phlox-eyed with lavender.

'Filigree' is one of the few small-growing geraniums with tri-color foliage. In addition to this asset, it yields salmon-pink, single flowers.

'Fleurette' displays its vibrant, deep salmon, double flowers on a stocky, dwarf plant that is covered with zoned leaves of black-green. This variety blooms well over a long period.

'Goblin' is a vigorous-growing miniature with double flowers of glowing red. These are close-set in the umbels, and the plant as a whole is compact and desirable.

'Imp' is one of the smallest miniature geraniums. Its shady, dark foliage contrasts with crisp single flowers of salmon-pink.

ILLUSTRATION 36. 'Mme. Fournier' miniature geranium, sometimes called 'Scarlet Pimpernel,' is a prolific, old variety. It has very dark green leaves and small, single, scarlet flowers. (Scale: 2-inch pot.)

'Kiffa' has double flowers with petals sometimes curled and twisted. They are pale pink-white at the edges, changing to rich pink toward the centers. This variety is a miniature, maturing at 6 inches or less, and producing leaves of plain green without any zonal marking.

'Kleiner Liebling' ("Little Darling") may reward its owner with umbels of pink flowers when it is less than 3 inches tall. Its leaves are like a typical zonal geranium, though not deeply marked. This variety stays small and blooms without ceasing. It is well-branched, and the bright, clean appearance of the foliage gives it value whether used as a container plant, or propagated to use in the outdoor garden during warm weather. 'Kleiner Liebling Variegated' has green and white foliage, but is otherwise the same.

'Lilliput Lemon' or *Pelargonium crispum minor* is a miniature with lemon-scented crinkled leaves. It is particularly choice for a collection of small geraniums, since so few of the scented-leaf varieties are dwarf enough to be suitable.

'Merope' (or 'Black Dwarf') has black-red, double flowers, foiled by dark foliage. The leaves are typical of a large zonale geranium, except they are less than an inch in diameter. In a year's time this variety will form a branched framework of brown, old-looking stems—like an ancient tree that has stood many a storm. Merry Gardens considers 'Merope' their best dark red miniature.

'Meteor' has dark red, double flowers with forest-green foliage that is banded by a deep, purple-black ring. It forms a compact, miniature plant of branching habit that blooms profusely (see Illustration 36).

'Minx' has an almost endless array of purple-crimson, double flowers. A new variety, this is one of the best miniature geraniums. It forms a dense, compact plant that is composed of sturdy stems and shady green, ruffled foliage.

'Pigmy' has wee semidouble flowers of bright red. These grow on one of the smallest of the miniature geraniums; a plant with apple-green, scalloped leaves on stems that branch of their own accord, but stay in a compact mound under 6 inches.

'Polaris' has umbels of white, pink-edged, single blooms. The small, dark leaves grow on miniature plants that branch and form neat mounds.

'Red Comet' is a miniature to be valued both for its foliage and its flowers. The leaves have a butterfly zone of black-green, and the narrow flower petals of cherry red have a white eye at their base. They form an airy umbel that is showy and graceful.

ILLUSTRATION 37. *'Night and Day' miniature geranium is a semi-dwarf variety with small, dark green leaves and light pink to white flowers. Very prolific. (Scale: 2-inch pot.)*

'Robin Hood' is a vigorous-growing semidwarf with double flowers of bright, clear red. Its leaves of grass green have a reddish brown zone. The plants flower in great profusion; they are sometimes covered with bloom. It is recommended for outdoor use in the summer, for the flowers and leaves come through the heat without any sunburning.

'Rosy Dawn' has double flowers with twisted petals of vibrant apricot or orange-red. They appear on a plant of dark green, zoned foliage. Even after a year or more, this plant will remain a true miniature—compact and occupying the space you allocated for it in the beginning.

'Ruffles' may bloom at 2 inches and stays very miniature. It has semidouble, ruffled flowers of light salmon.

'Salmon Comet' has single flowers that are narrow-petaled and salmon in color. These appear freely, foiled by wee leaves that are attractively marked by a butterfly zone. Miniature (see Illustration 35).

'Sirius' has salmon-pink flowers that shade to white in the center. They are airy and small, but what they lack in size they make up for in quantity. Miniature.

'Sleepy' is a semidwarf plant that bears braggadocio single blooms of salmon-pink.

'Small Fortune' has white, double flowers that are marked in the center with pink. These appear freely on a compact, bushy miniature plant.

'Snow White' is of easy culture with large single white flowers over dark green foliage.

'Sorcery' has a widely zoned leaf on stems that have a spreading habit. Freely produces single, orange-scarlet flowers. Recommended for hanging baskets.

'Sparkle' is a sturdy-growing semidwarf with dark foliage and quantities of glowing rose-red, double flowers.

'Tiberius' has dark pink, double flowers above dark green foliage. It blooms well.

'Tiny Tim,' in this case a miniature geranium, not the popular midget tomato by the same name, has single red flowers with tiny individual leaves of dark black-green. Available also with pink flowers (see Illustration 35).

ILLUSTRATION 38. *'Snow Baby' miniature geranium. (Scale: leaf 1 inch across.)*

ILLUSTRATION 39. *'Sugar Baby' miniature ivyleaf geranium. (Scale: leaf 1 inch across.)*

'Tweedledee' is a semidwarf with dark ginkgo-like scalloped leaves. They are zoned attractively also. The robust, branching plant produces single, narrow-petaled flowers of light salmon.

'Tweedledum' is similar in appearance to 'Tweedledee,' except it has flowers of a darker shade of salmon.

'Twinkle' is a semidwarf with dark foliage and double flowers of rose-pink.

'Urchin' has dark green leaves that are narrow and twisted. The semidouble flowers have poinsettia or cactus form, dark red. A good bloomer and unusual.

'Volcano' is a true miniature with small zonale leaves of dark black-green, and large, single, vivid crimson blooms (Illustration 35).

'Zip' has a distinctly zoned leaf, with large, single cerise flowers. An excellent miniature.

ILLUSTRATION 40. *'Zip' miniature geranium. (Scale: 2-inch pot.)*

8. Miniature and Compact English Ivies

Indoors and outdoors, English ivy is one of the most useful of all plants. The best varieties for house and greenhouse are those that are naturally miniature or semidwarf. My favorite ivies are described at the end of this chapter; a collector would enjoy them all.

To us who find plants fascinating, English ivy is more than a vine with attractive foliage. For one thing it is an evergreen that attaches itself and climbs by means of aerial roots that sprout along the stems. *Hedera* is dimorphic, that is, it grows in two forms—first in a juvenile state, then as an adult. The second stage is usually not reached until the plant has grown to the top of a rough-barked tree trunk or rock wall—a height of at least 10 feet. Then it passes into adulthood. The aerial roots cease to appear and the ivy becomes bushy. The leaves change shape, too, and clusters of dainty, white flowers are produced, usually in the fall. Bess Shippy, *Hedera* expert, reports that in recent years she has had flowers on a number of pot-grown English ivies.

🌿 Origin of New English Ivies

Most if not all new English ivies originate as sports or muta-tions which appear frequently. If you grow ivy successfully for several years, chances are you will have the pleasure of seeing at least one branch grow partially or entirely different from the rest of the plant. To propagate this maverick, clip it from the parent plant and root it as a cutting.

English ivy merits lavish planting in house and greenhouse. Grow it in clay or plastic pots, with or without the support of a trellis or totem pole. Plant it in redwood, wire, or other type of hanging basket, or cultivate the true miniature or semi-dwarfs in a strawberry jar. Root a number of cuttings in the fall in order to have quantities of potted ivies for window boxes in spring and summer. Since light late frosts won't harm it, the ivy can be planted out several weeks ahead of petunias, geraniums, and other window-box plants.

🌿 English Ivy Trees

The most interesting way to grow English ivy is to train it to tree form. The size and shape of the tree is up to you—a tiny one of miniature ivy, or an impressive tree 2 to 3 feet tall. The shape may be that of a globe, a pyramid, or a cone. Here is the way to do it: Make a framework of 1-inch chicken wire or similar material. Fill it with coarse sphagnum moss which has been moistened with liquid fertilizer, such as 23-21-17. Then secure the base of the form in a pot of moist soil (the same mixture you use for other ivies). Plant rooted cuttings of ivy at intervals all around between the pot and the base of the framework. Train the cuttings to cover the form; the stems may be hairpinned to the moss until they root into it. Soak the moss often enough to keep it barely moist. After the tree form has been covered, routine pruning will keep it tailored to the same proportions for an indefinite time. Turn the tree every few days so that all sides receive equal light.

🍃 How To Grow

Few plants grow as readily as English ivy. Cold-hardiness makes it superior for growing in a window that gets chilly at night. Even when humidity condenses on the window and freezes into ice, the ivy on the sill thrives. In spite of this enthusiastic introduction to ivy culture, I must give one warning: If the soil in which ivy is growing is allowed to dry out for more than a few days, plants will die. Ivy can also be killed by allowing the roots to stand for days in a water-logged condition.

Outdoors, English ivy thrives in good garden soil—one that is moderately fertile, enriched with humus and well-drained. This same soil is not such a good choice for potted ivy. The best growing medium for container-grown ivies consists of three parts screened sphagnum moss to one of fine-grained horticultural perlite. Ivies growing in this mixture should be fertilized once a month with some well-balanced house plant fertilizer, as 23-21-17. Or a mixture of equal parts garden loam, vermiculite, and peat moss will grow good ivy. Commercial or homemade mediums for African violets will also produce satisfactory ivy. If ivy is planted in rich, humusy soil, it will need no additional plant food for several months. Otherwise apply fertilizer once a month or use one of the new timed-release foods such as Precise according to directions on the container.

As house or greenhouse plants, ivies do well in bright, open shade or with up to several hours of full sunlight, particularly during the fall and winter. When ivy is receiving enough light, the stems are sturdy and the foliage is a bright, healthy green. Without sufficient light, spaces between leaves elongate and growth is spindly, foliage a pale green. Such a condition also results from too much heat, lack of humidity, or too dry soil.

Ivy grows best in a container with a drainage hole. If you find it necessary to use an undrained pot, plant the ivy in light, well-aerated soil, such as Black Magic Planter Mix, or in a mixture of three parts screened sphagnum moss to one of perlite. Water frequently to saturate the earth ball. Then immediately remove any excess. Avoid a flood followed by drought.

Under average house conditions, ivies should be particularly well watered at least once a week. Set the plant in sink or baththub, cover the soil with a piece of polyethylene plastic, and then shower the foliage above and beneath with clean water, preferably of room temperature. It is important to remember that a window which is humid in summer may be arid whenever the weather is cold enough to have the furnace on. The hotter and drier the atmosphere, the more frequently ivy should be showered.

If the surface of ivy leaves gets white- or yellow-flecked and tiny webs appear underneath and in the axils of the leaves, minute red spider mites are probably present. When English ivy is kept adequately moist and the air is reasonably fresh and humid, red spider mites should not appear, but sometimes in spite of seemingly perfect conditions, it may be necessary to use a miticide at 7- to 10-day intervals until there are no further signs of mites. If possible, dip the ivy in the miticide (mixed precisely according to package directions); otherwise, spray with it.

Brown scale sometimes infests ivy. A single mature scale appears as a tan-colored oval about an eighth of an inch long. Scale first feeds on the underside of leaves, but as it multiplies, all leaf surfaces and also stems may be covered. A larger plant infested with scale should be dipped in a pail of malathion; a small one may be dipped in malathion, or sprayed with a house-plant insecticide. Repeat weekly until no scale remains.

🐜 Propagation of Ivy

Ivy is propagated by cuttings. Take growing tips, 3 to 4 inches long or, if conditions are ideal, root pieces of stem that include one leaf node above. From this, new growth will sprout. Take a tip cutting using a sharp knife. Strip off the lower inch or two of leaves. Then insert the bare portion of the stem into a moist rooting medium, such as sand or a half-and-half combination of peat moss and sand. Tip cuttings of miniature ivies may be much shorter—an inch above the soil, with one or two leaf nodes inserted into the medium. For quick rooting, ivies need a moist atmosphere of 62 to 72 degrees and bright light. Cover the cuttings with moisture-preserving polyethylene plastic, fruit jars, or drinking glasses until new growth begins.

FAVORITE IVIES FOR THE COLLECTOR

'California Gold' is compact, bushy, and self-branching. The pale green leaves are heavily splashed with golden yellow.

'Curlilocks' branches and grows large at a rapid pace. The bold, curled leaves measure 1½ by 2 inches. They are fluted and ruffled and bright apple green in color.

'Fan' is a small, branching ivy. It is not a miniature, but it can be pruned and trained to small proportions. The slight fluting of this foliage is particularly pleasing; it does not distort the typical ivy shape, but rather embellishes and distinguishes it.

'Garland,' like many ivies, is prone to produce leaves that have considerable variance from one to another. Some are elongated hearts; others are three-lobed. They may be clipped and trained to form a compact plant.

'Glacier' has variegated, small triangular green, gray and white leaves of intermediate size. It is not as large as the English ivy grown outdoors, but not nearly as small as such miniatures as 'Needlepoint.'

'Glymii' has small leaves set on a stiff trailing stem. They are sometimes spooned.

'Gold Heart' has small leaves of fresh green with a bright center of golden yellow. Alone or in a combination with a plain ivy, such as 'Merion Beauty,' this variety is one of the most striking.

'Green Feather,' has perhaps the smallest of all ivy leaves. They are set one on top of the other along the stems, and the plant has a feathery appearance. This is sometimes offered as *Hedera Helix* var. *meagheri*.

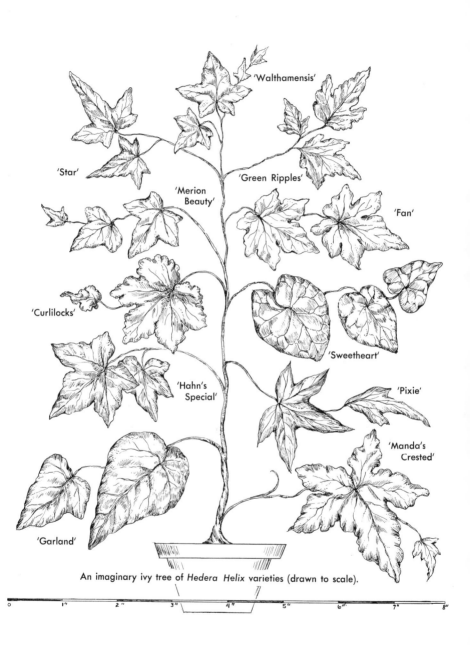

'Walthamensis'

'Star'

'Green Ripples'

'Merion
Beauty'

'Fan'

'Curlilocks'

'Sweetheart'

'Hahn's
Special'

'Pixie'

'Manda's
Crested'

'Garland'

An imaginary ivy tree of *Hedera Helix* varieties (drawn to scale).

0   1"   2"   3"   4"   5"   6"   7"   8"

ILLUSTRATION 41. *An imaginary tree of miniature English ivies.*

ILLUSTRATION 42. Hedera helix 'Glacier.' *(Scale: 3-inch pot.)*

'Green Ripples' has small arrowhead leaves to 1 inch in length. They grow on a semiminiature, branching plant.

'Green Spear' is a small-growing ivy, similar to 'Merion Beauty' in size. The lance-shaped or arrowhead leaves vary considerably, but they are close-set on the stems and the plant as a whole is excellent.

'Hahn's' is, in all respects, one of the loveliest ivies. The medium-sized leaves have a noticeable network of silver veins. They are about 1 inch wide by 1½ inches long. A compact, bushy plant of deep green.

'Jubilee' is a miniature variegated ivy with striking leaves, many of them entirely cream-white. Some are edged with cream-white; others are marbled all over with dark green, silver-gray and cream-white.

'Manda's Crested' has star-shaped leaves that are fluted and lobed; at maturity they may be 2½ to 3 inches across. Not small-growing, but it can be kept compact by clipping and training. Delightful when grown to tree form.

'Merion Beauty' is a rapid-growing miniature. Widely available, it is one of the loveliest and most easily grown ivies. Small leaves vary in shape, but in general they are the typical form of English ivy, less than 1 inch in diameter.

ILLUSTRATION 43. Hedera helix *'Merion Beauty'* with standard *English ivy—to show comparison of leaf sizes.*

'Needlepoint' (also called 'Itsy Bitsy') is a true miniature, branching ivy. Leaves measure 1 by 1 inch overall, but they are deeply cut into five lobes. This will grow for a year or more in a 2½-inch pot.

'Pedata' has deeply-cut, five-lobed leaves shaped like a bird's foot. It forms a beautiful, long and graceful vine. Particularly oustanding for hanging baskets and window boxes.

'Pixie' is a choice, branching ivy. The individual leaves have a beautiful shape; they measure 1¼ by 1 inch at maturity.

'Star' is a small-growing ivy that branches and trails to form a pleasing mound of green. Leaves are close-set, and the plant as a whole is choice.

'Sweetheart' has leaves of perfect heart shape 1 inch in diameter, deep green, and veined with a striking mosaic of silver. Although a medium to large size ivy, this can be pruned and trained to small proportions.

'Walthamensis' is a petite ivy, not as small as 'Needlepoint,' but considered a miniature. The leaves, of typical ivy shape, have prominent silver-white veining. It grows quickly, climbs well by aerial roots, and is a good choice for planting as an ivy tree.

Besides these favorite English ivies which I have grown through the years, ivy experts Bess Shippy and Mary Ellen Ross suggest these:

caenwoodiana
conglomerata prostrata
'Emerald Jewel'
'Fleur de Lis'
'Holly'
'Irish Lace'
'Ivalace'
'Knobby' (stems twist; try as a bonsai)
'Little Diamond'
'Marmorata' (*H. h. discolor*)
'Plume d'Or'
sagittaefolia variegata
'Shamrock'
'Sinclair Silver Leaf'
'Shannon'
'Telecurl'

9. Miniature Orchids

Plant collectors report more than 30,000 different orchids, and at least 15,000 of these have been identified as to species. I am told that there are hundreds, perhaps thousands, of miniature orchids. In my recommendations of orchids, I have had in mind their availability at reasonable prices in this country. You will discover, I am sure, that one miniature orchid leads to another; buy your first and you'll be on your way to one of the most fascinating and rewarding of plant hobbies.

It is a fair question as to how small an orchid must be to be considered a miniature. I draw the line at 10 inches except for two or three irresistible exceptions! And these are still relatively small, and even a 10-inch plant may seem a giant when placed beside orchids that mature at 2 inches with flowers less than 1 inch across.

To do justice to the orchids, and your own high hopes, know something about culture before you start. My discussion here covers general needs. In the individual descriptions that follow, more explicit instructions are given. To become really successful with orchids, read a book or so devoted exclusively to them, and study the catalogs of specialists. You would also enjoy membership in the American Orchid Society. (Annual dues are $12.50; the address of the society is in care of the Botanical Museum of Harvard University, Cambridge, Massachusetts 02138.)

🦎 Containers and Humidity

Orchids, unlike many miniature plants, do not grow well in unusual containers. Even though they are diminutive, they must be handled just like the larger types. So you will need a supply of standard orchid clay pots, chunks of treefern or osmunda fiber, orchid compost, fertilizer (as offered by orchid growers), hanging baskets and pot hangers.

Orchids need a moist atmosphere; 55 to 70 per cent humidity is a prerequisite. With the aid of a humidity guide, determine the percentage of relative humidity in the area where you plan to grow them. Of course, it is easier to provide humidity for miniature orchids than for large ones. For example, you can group several miniatures in a terrarium (Illustration 44). I have eight different ones in 2½- and 3-inch pots growing inside a former aquarium that measures 8 inches wide by 16 inches long by 10 inches deep. This unit is effective, easily fitted into a plant collection, lightweight, attractive and inexpensive. Such a case should not be closed completely, for, if it is, the air becomes stale for the orchids. When the air is very dry, however, it is a good idea to place a glass or polyethylene cover over the opening in the case leaving the cover open an inch or two to permit circulation of air.

A practical way to increase humidity is to set plants on trays filled with pebbles that are kept wet. Or for a few miniatures, you can use a small glass baking dish. For a number of plants, have a 2-inch-deep galvanized tray made to hold them. Some enthusiasts simply fill a shallow pan with water, put a wire rack salvaged from an oven or refrigerator over it, and then set the pots on this. Whatever the method, be certain that the base of a pot never rests in water. It takes ages to kill an orchid by drought, but they drown quickly.

ILLUSTRATION 44. *A terrarium of miniature orchids. Left to right:* Ornithocephalus bicornis, *2 inches tall; foliage of* Mystacidium distichum; *a young plant of* Ludisia discolor *(formerly* Haemaria discolor dawsonia) *with flowers; and* Oncidium triquetrum *in flower. The two pots of trailing, ferny growth are* Selaginella kraussiana.

Growing Medium

Although orchids need a moist atmosphere, they require fresh air. They will not thrive in stagnant air that does not circulate. At the other extreme—as in a drafty cold place or in hot dry wind—they will not do well either.

Usually we think of orchids as being epiphytes—plants that obtain most of their nourishment from the air. In the wild, the epiphytic orchids grow in the crotches of trees or wherever they find a humusy place to lodge. During a rain and immediately after they have an abundant water supply. However, as the sun comes out and the wind blows, the orchid roots dry and so remain until the next rain. Although the roots may be dry, the atmosphere around them is not. This is an important point to remember in growing epiphytes. In containers, epiphytic orchids are potted in osmunda fiber, redwood bark, shredded fir or treefern from Central America.

Some orchids are terrestrials, that is, they grow in humusy soil. As pot plants, they are planted in peat moss or in mixtures of sphagnum moss, osmunda fiber, shredded pine bark and loam. The planting medium varies for different genera. Where possible, I have recommended mixtures in the descriptions of the plants.

When you water the growing medium of an orchid, soak it well. Set the pot in a pan of water and when it is so saturated that the top soil feels moist, remove it, allow it to drain, and then return it to the growing place. The plant does not need water again until the sides of the pot feel dry, and plant and pot are lightweight when you lift them.

On bright, sunny days, syringe foliage as often as possible. Aim the mist at the foliage and stop before it collects to the point of draining into the soil. It is also beneficial to wash foliage. Use a soft cotton cloth and water of room temperature. If this is done carefully and frequently, insects should not bother you. However, regular spraying with an orchid insecticide is a safety precaution, particularly for a large collection.

⊱ Light Requirements

Some orchids like the *Odontoglossum* are shade plants. These thrive in bright light and do not need hot, direct sun. If you are growing such orchids as house plants, they will do well in an east window through fall and winter, except, possibly in the semi-tropics. When a plantsman classifies an orchid as shade loving, he is thinking of the bright light of open shade outdoors, not deep dark shade. During spring and summer, shade-loving orchids will do better in north light, or outdoors in shade. Many orchids like the *Oncidium* need filtered or dappled sunlight to grow and flower well. This is the type of light they receive in the wild, as on the branch of a tree. Thus, the more light an orchid species needs, the higher it would grow on a tree. A good rule of thumb with orchids is to give all the light possible, but not to the point of causing foliage to turn yellow.

For best results, three temperature ranges are suggested for orchids indoors: cool with a minimum night temperature of 50 degrees F., intermediate or moderate with a night temperature of 55 to 65 degrees F., and warm with a night minimum of 60 to 65 degrees F. A rise of 5 to 20 degrees may be expected during the day, and perhaps more than that in the heat of summer.

In a collection of orchids, keep the miniatures by themselves, or in some way set them apart. Otherwise, a plant may get permanently lost if it is accidentally pushed behind some towering giant—a standard orchid could easily keep a precious miniature from the attention it needs.

🌿 Orchids Under Fluorescent Lights

If you have no window space or greenhouse in which to grow miniature orchids, grow them under fluorescent lights. Suspend a standard commercial unit over a table, placing the tubes about 18 inches above the table. Three 40-watt daylight tubes in a 15-inch reflector will provide excellent light for a table 24 inches wide by 48 inches long. There are several types of fluorescent tubes, and there have been numerous recommendations about using the right combination of these for growing plants. I have tried various tubes, and all of them have yielded good results. For the sake of simplicity, I have all daylight tubes. Perhaps the more important thing is to use fresh tubes; for maximum results, replace them every six months. Orchids growing under fluorescent lights respond best to 12 to 14 hours of illumination out of every 24. Give seedlings up to 18 hours out of every 24 and they will bloom a year or so sooner.

🌿 OUTSTANDING MINIATURE ORCHIDS

Acampe pachyglossa grows 4 to 8 inches tall and has ¾-inch flowers of yellow, striped with a bright, reddish color. These appear in the summer or fall, growing in a fluffy 3-inch ball atop a short stem. Likes to be slightly damp in sunny warmth.

Aerides japonicum (Illustration 45), grows 4 to 10 inches tall, has fragrant white flowers that are striped transversely with purple, is summer-blooming. It requires partial sunlight, moist osmunda fiber as a growing medium, and a temperature of 60 to 85 degrees F.

ILLUSTRATION 45. Aerides japoni-cum, *miniature orchid.*

ILLUSTRATION 46. Cattleya walkeri-ana, *miniature orchid. Photograph courtesy Rod McLellan Company.*

Ascocentrum ampullaceum grows 4 to 6 inches tall, has rose-purple flowers ½ to 1 inch across. These may appear from March to June on a short upright spike. The plant needs a warm, humid place in partial sunlight and moist osmunda. *A. miniatum* grows 4 to 8 inches tall, has ½- to ¾-inch flowers of clear yellow-gold, orange-red, or coral; they may come from January to June, sometimes in October.

Cattleya aclandiae grows 6 to 8 inches tall. The flowers come in the summer and vary from 3 to 4 inches in diameter. The sepals and petals are yellow-green, spotted with brownish purple; the lip of the flower is magenta-purple. The plant is creeping and does best in a shallow pot. *C. luteola* grows to nine inches, and any time from November to August bears clusters of rich yellow flowers.

C. walkeriana (Illustration 46), has very fragrant rose flowers up to 5 inches in diameter on a plant 4 to 6 inches tall. These, as other cattleyas, are epiphytes. They require a moderate temperature, humidity, filtered sunlight and a grow-ing medium of osmunda that is allowed to become dry be-tween waterings.

ILLUSTRATION 47. Dendrobium kentrophyllum. *(Scale: 3-inch pot.)* *Photograph courtesy Alberts & Merkel Bros., Inc.*

ILLUSTRATION 48. Ludisia discolor, *a beautiful foliage orchid. (Scale: 2-inch pot.)*

Chondrorphyncha wendtlandii grows 6 to 9 inches tall and in the fall bears large flowers that appear singly on short stems. These are creamy white with a bluish lip. Plants need a growing medium of moist osmunda, a moderate temperature and a humid atmosphere in dappled sunlight.

Cymbidium ensifolium (2-inch flowers of yellow-green or sepia, shading to white) and *C. pumilum* are cataloged by some growers as miniatures for 4- or 5-inch pots, though they exceed my 10-inch limit by as much as 8 inches or more. However, because some of the new miniature hybrid cymbidiums such as 'Bo Peep,' 'Piso,' 'Flirtation' and 'Peter Pan' are so desirable, I have included them here. Cymbidiums cannot stand hot, stuffy conditions at any time. I recommend them only for those who have well-ventilated, air-conditioned greenhouses.

Dendrobium aggregatum grows to 5 inches and in the spring yields spikes of yellow blooms. During the fall and early winter it should have a drier atmosphere, less water and a bit cooler—even into the 50s at night. Culture is as for cattleya, except with more warmth. *D. jenkinsii* grows about

2 inches tall, and is undoubtedly one of the best miniatures. The bright golden yellow 1½-inch flowers grow singly, or to a cluster of three on a stem. *D. loddigesi* has lavender-pink flowers. *D. monile* grows to 6 inches in height and produces pairs of pure white, fragrant flowers at each node along the pseudobulb.

Epidendrum polybulbon grows about 4 inches tall, and from September to April, and possibly June or July, it bears ¾-inch flowers of yellow and brown. The lip is white, marked with yellow.

Laelia pumila grows to 8 inches tall. It has beautiful rounded blooms of rose-purple with a lip of purplish crimson. These appear in the fall, sometimes into winter. The plant likes a cool, moist atmosphere in partial sunlight and needs to become dry between waterings.

Lockhartia oerstedii might well be grown just for its attractive foliage. The leaves enfold an upright stem, and appear as if they had been braided. It may bloom at any time with flowers of red-spotted yellow. *L. pallida* is similar but has flowers of creamy, pale yellow. These need a growing medium of osmunda that is allowed to dry out between waterings; they must have good drainage, and a location in partial sunlight that is warm and humid. Use relatively small clay pots, or mount on chunks of treefern.

Ludisia discolor (formerly *Haemaria discolor dawsoniana*)— see Illustration 48—is, at maturity, not a miniature. However, it is grown primarily for its foliage, and as such a plant, it may be maintained in a 3-inch pot for at least a year. It is a perfect subject for a terrarium that receives some ventilation, but where the air is warm (60 to 65 degrees at night) and free from hot, dry, or cold drafts. Alberts and Merkel Brothers recommend a potting mixture of equal parts cut osmunda and sphagnum moss with some finely crushed charcoal and a few screened oak leaves. The leaves of this orchid are a dark, vibrant shade of wine-green, and they are lined with definite veinings of reddish or pinkish green.

Maxillaria fredrickstahlii grows 3 or 4 inches tall and bears ½-inch flowers of pale yellow with a darker lip that sometimes has a greenish cast. It grows easily in a moderate temperature if it has a humid atmosphere, some sunlight and moist osmunda.

Mystacidium distichum (sometimes classified as an *Angraecum*) is a small epiphyte, to 9 inches, that sends its upside-down flowers out of the axils of the tightly plaited foliage. These appear in late summer and early autumn. Treat as a cattleya, except it can stand more warmth (see Illustration 44).

Neofinetia falcata (Illustration 49), sometimes listed as *Angraecum falcatum*, grows 3 to 6 inches tall and bears fragrant, long-lasting flowers of pure white. These have slender spurs, about 2 inches long, that give the spikes of flowers an airy, spidery effect. This orchid likes a cool (an average of 60 degrees is ideal), moist place that receives some filtered sunlight and moist osmunda fiber.

Odontoglossum rossii grows to about 6 inches tall and bears winter blooms 2 to 3 inches across. They are rose-flushed white with spots of dark brown. This orchid likes a cool, humid place in the shade and moist osmunda. *O. krameri* bears scapes of three violet flowers, the lip of each marked with a distinct narrow band of dark brown near the column. It grows from 4 to 8 inches tall, and forms a plant of bright, grass green.

ILLUSTRATION 49. Neofinetia falcata, *miniature orchid.* ILLUSTRATION 50. Oncidium triquetrum, *miniature orchid.*

Oncidium cheirophorum grows 4 to 8 inches tall, and is undoubtedly one of the loveliest miniatures. It bears sprays of flowers from October to December. They are of brightest yellow and appear in thick clusters. The plant likes to be cool, particularly after blooming. It needs a moist atmosphere with partial sunlight and should be allowed to become dry between waterings. *O. iridifolium*, sometimes called *O. pusillum*, grows 3 inches tall, and in the summer bears dime-sized flowers of red-spotted pale yellow. The foliage grows in a fan shape like a garden iris. *O. tetrapetalum* grows 3 to 6 inches tall and produces sprays of white and brown flowers in the summer. *O. triquetrum* (see Illustrations 44 and 50) grows 3 to 5 inches tall and produces late winter and early spring flowers of yellow, white, and brownish red. *O. ornythorhynchum* may send its sprays of flowers up to 18 inches (August to early winter), but they are fragrant, and a luscious color of soft rosy lilac, with a yellow crest—so choice that the height is forgivable. *O. pulchellum* is similar in size to *O. ornytho-rhynchum* but has scapes of rose-flushed white flowers in the summer. *O. variegatum*, a miniature, has leaves of forest green, spotted with wine-red. The large (for a plant so small) flowers are white with cheerful red markings. These 1-inch blooms appear on a scape that may overshadow the 6-inch foliage by almost 12 inches. *Oncidium longiflorum* (Illustration 51) has buttercup-yellow and maple-brown flowers an inch across in the spring and early summer. These, including the pseudobulbs and leaves, do not exceed 4 inches. All of the more succulent oncidiums do best mounted on slabs or chunks of treefern.

Ornithocephalus bicornis grows 2 inches tall, and produces a miniature iris-like fan of foliage. The greenish-white flowers appear in the winter and sometimes in other seasons. To fully appreciate them, you will need a magnifying glass. This orchid likes a shaded, humid place, a moderate temperature and moist osmunda (see Illustration 44).

Paphiopedilum concolor grows to 6 inches tall and produces a strikingly plain flower of pale yellow that is misted with tiny violet dots. The blooming time is August or September. This is a terrestrial orchid that does well in a warm place that is shaded and humid. It needs a growing medium of moist humus. Some growers use peat moss and fertilize every four weeks with a completely balanced orchid food, such as one with an analysis of 20-20-20. *P. fairieanum* grows to 6 inches tall and produces fall and winter flowers that are an unusual combination of white, shaded with yellow-green, veined with purple. *P. bellatulum* may grow to 10 inches, but is still classified by most growers as a dwarf. It has shell-shaped, waxen, cream flowers up to 3 inches in diameter, spotted with maroon, and set off by green foliage that is mottled with purple carried through from the undersides of the leaves. The paphiopedilums are the indoor counterpart to the outdoor ladyslipper orchids, the cypripediums. In fact, many catalogs list the paphiopedilums as cypripediums.

Phalaenopsis equestris, sometimes called *P. rosea*, grows to 8 inches tall. The flower sepals and petals are white flushed with rose-pink at their base, and the lip is rose-purple. It thrives in a warm, humid place that receives bright light, but not necessarily direct sunlight, and needs a growing medium of moist osmunda.

ILLUSTRATION 51. Oncidium longi-florum, *miniature orchid.*

ILLUSTRATION 52. Oncidium *equitant hybrid, miniature orchid. (Scale: leaf span 5 inches.)*

Physosiphon tubatus grows 6 to 8 inches tall, and produces a raceme of bright orange flowers. These appear anytime from November to August. The leaves of this orchid form a compact turf. It is an epiphyte and thrives in coolness where it has humidity. Plant in moist osmunda and place where it does not receive direct sunlight.

Pleurothallis picta grows about 2 inches tall and bears orange flowers set off by oval, fleshy leaves that are closely set on the stem. Plant in moist osmunda and grow in an intermediate temperature. Provide filtered light and moist but fresh air. *P. fulgens* has bright red flowers. One grower has suggested this growing medium for *P. fulgens*: three parts osmunda, two parts sphagnum, and one part leaf mold. It would be a good idea to try it for *P. picta* and *P. grobyi*, another miniature of this generic name, that has yellow and crimson flowers.

Rodriguezia fragrans is a rare and choice miniature orchid. It bears yellow-lipped white flowers up to 1¼ inches in diameter. This plant will do well in a mixture of equal parts sphagnum moss and osmunda. It needs warmth (a minimum of 60 degrees), moisture in the summer, but just barely damp in the winter and shade during hot weather. *R. secunda* has an arching flower stem (to 15 inches) that is set with a double row of small rose-pink flowers in the spring; perhaps not quite a miniature, but a good choice anyway.

Schomburgkia thompsoniana reaches maturity at 6 to 8 inches, but begins to bloom when scarcely 3 inches tall. It produces long bloom stems, however, up to 30 inches in length, with 2½-inch flowers of creamy yellow. It needs full sunlight in the winter and should be grown in osmunda or bark that is watered and fed heavily in the spring and summer, but not so much the rest of the year.

Sophronitis coccinea, sometimes called *S. grandiflora*, grows 3 to 6 inches tall, and produces vivid orange-red, 2-inch flowers in the winter. It needs a cool, moist place that receives filtered sunlight. Plant in moist osmunda.

In addition to the small-growing orchids already suggested, grower Jean Merkel of Alberts & Merkel Brothers, suggests these: *Dendrochilum uncatum, Oncidium henekenii* 'Bumble Bee' and hybrids such as Queen Bee and Red Belt, *Phalaenopsis lueddemanniana purpurea* and *pulchra* and their hybrids, *Phalaenopsis amboinensis* and *Pholidota chinensis.*

The current catalog of Jones and Scully includes a listing of "little somethings"—which they bill as "fascinating compacts, to grow in next-to-nothing space." Besides some of the small orchids already discussed in this chapter, they list these miniatures ("which grow to maturity in 3- or 4-inch pots, not over 8 inches tall"):

Aerangis articulata
Aerangis citrata
Aerangis stylosa
Aerides godefroyana
Aerides maculosa
Angraecum chloranthum
Angraecum philippinense
Ascocentrum hendersonianum
Asocentrum micranthum
Broughtonia sanguinea
Dendrobium canaliculatum
Dendrobium jenkinsii
Dendrobium leonis
Epidendrum mariae
Epidendrum porpax
Erycina echinata
Gastrochilus acutifolium
Gastrochilus bellinus
Gastrochilus calceolare
Gastrochilus dasypogon
Gomesa crispa
Gomesa recurva
Leptotes bicolor
Leptotes unicolor

Notylia barkeri
Oncidium bifolium
Oncidium bifolium
   var. *majus*
Oncidium desertorum
Oncidium haitiense
Oncidium onustum
Oncidium pumilum
Oncidium stramineum
Oncidium uniflorum var.
   longipes
Ornithocephalus
   cochleariformis
Paphiopedilum godefroyae
Paphiopedilum niveum
Paphiopedilum niveum
   'Ang Thong'
Paphiopedilum sukhakulii
Phalaenopsis parishii
Rodriguezia decora
Rodriguezia venusta
Saccolabium quisumbingii
Sarcochilus ceciliae
   var. *roseus*

10. Miniature Roses

Miniature roses are pure enchantment. They are tiny replicas of hybrid tea and floribunda roses with perfectly formed buds no bigger than a fat grain of wheat, and fragrant, nickel- to quarter-size flowers that appear continuously on plants 4 to 14 inches tall. Foliage, stems and thorns are also like that of standard rose plants except that they are smaller and more delicate. Besides miniature roses in bush, climbing and tree forms (some only 10 inches tall), there are now old-fashioned moss types and soon there will be trailers for hanging baskets and those with striped petals.

Miniature roses require all possible sunlight through fall and winter—preferably at an unshaded south window. In summer on a window sill or in a window box, they will thrive in an east or west exposure.

If you have no sunny place for miniature roses, grow them under fluorescent lights. Use a standard commercial unit with 13- or 15-inch reflector and two or three 40-watt daylight or Gro-Lux tubes. Suspend this 4 to 6 inches above the plants and burn the lights 16 hours out of every 24. After a few weeks of blooming, buds may reach into the light tubes. Then either lower the plant, or raise the lights; or, and this is preferable, shear the whole plant back to 3 inches from the soil. It will respond by quickly pushing forth compact new growth and many buds. Two of the best varieties to grow under lights, according to grower and breeder Ralph Moore, are 'White Angel' and 'Yellow Jewel.'

In addition to sunshine or fluorescent light, miniature roses need humidity. The ideal moisture-temperature ratio for human beings—50 per cent humidity and 72-degree F. temperature—will also grow floriferous and healthy miniature roses. More humidity, even 60 to 70 per cent, is desirable so long as the air is fresh, not stale and close as it may be inside a terrarium. To provide miniature roses with moisture-laden air, group them with other house plants on a tray of moist sand, pebbles, coarse vermiculite, perlite or peat moss. Where temperatures and humidity are high, some gentle air circulation is a big help.

Where To Obtain

Miniature roses are now available at most garden centers, or you can get them by mail all through the year (see list of suppliers in the back of the book). Since they are hardy outdoors, it is possible to ship them safely even in very cold weather. In winter, a miniature rose will come as a dormant bush without foliage. You can then plant it in a mixture of equal parts of loam, leaf mold, sand and well-rotted cow manure. A 5- or 6-inch bulb pan (the flat type of flower pot) is adequate for the roots of these small bushes. Most miniature roses are shipped as 2½- or 3-inch potted plants, and not bare root. Water well after repotting.

If you receive a miniature rose in early fall, after repotting, if possible, sink the pot in a protected place outdoors or in a cold frame, and leave it there until after Christmas. Then bring it to a sunny window in a room where the night temperature ranges from 60 to 65 degrees F. To stimulate the dormant canes into growth, cover the plant with a polyethylene bag or glass jar. This will keep the air moist. As soon as the leaf buds break and growth is obvious, gradually remove the protective covering over a period of five to seven days. This will harden the new growth to the outside air.

If it is impossible for you to put your potted miniature rose outdoors for a few weeks in the late fall, then place it directly in a sunny window, and encourage it to begin active growth at once.

If you obtain a miniature rose through the mail after Christmas, chances are it will have been dormant for a few weeks. It is then ready for warmth and sunlight. If you buy a miniature rose already in bloom, as at a spring flower show, immediately repot it in a container 1 to 2 inches larger in diameter than the one in which it has been growing. As flowers fade, prune and trim the bush to keep it shapely.

ILLUSTRATION 53.
Thimble and pen show just how small the miniature roses are.

Good ventilation discourages mildew on indoor roses. Fresh air should come from an open window in another room so that cold drafts will not strike the plant. When it is in active growth, keep the soil moist, but not dripping wet, and feed it every two or three weeks with a 5-10-5 liquid house plant fertilizer, following directions on the container.

If you pinch out the soft tip of new growth, a bushier plant will result, and eventually you will get more flowers. In sunny weather, spray the bush daily with water to increase humidity. Do this in the morning so that leaves will be dry by night, otherwise, you may encourage mildew.

🌿 Watch for Red Spider Mites

Red spider mites infest miniature roses grown in too high temperature and in low humidity. They may be present anyway, under the best of conditions. They fleck the leaves with white and may eventually reduce a plant to bare stems with a heap of yellow leaves at the base.

If red spiders infest your miniature roses, cut plants down to about 3 inches from the soil. Discard the trimmings, and spray stems and leaflets with a miticide. A special spray for

ILLUSTRATION 54. *'Green Ice' miniature rose has 1¼-inch flowers that open white or pale pink, then change to light green. Photograph courtesy Ralph Moore.*

roses that contains a fungicide, insecticide and miticide will solve a multitude of problems. After such drastic treatment for spider mites, improve the general growing conditions for your miniature roses. Try to increase the moisture content of the air, and check to see whether you are growing them in temperatures that constantly exceed 75 degrees F.

As an alternative to chopping off all growth, miniature rose grower and breeder Ernest Williams suggests this procedure: "With hand over top of pot, invert it and immerse the entire plant for 4 seconds in a miticide at spray strength."

🌿 Culture in Summer

If you have an outdoor garden, prune back your miniature roses in spring and plant them outside. If you plan to grow them indoors the following winter, keep them potted. Repotting can be done in spring or fall, but it should be attended to at least once a year. Knock off some of the old soil and repot in a new container, either of the same size or an inch or so larger.

ILLUSTRATION 55. 'Janice' miniature rose has dark pink buds and flowers. Blooms profusely. Photograph courtesy Ralph Moore.

ILLUSTRATION 56. *Bouquet of miniature roses shows how you can create the effect of having a large rose garden from which to select—yet all of these could be grown in one sunny window, or under fluorescent lights or in a fire-escape window box. Photograph courtesy Ralph Moore.*

☙ From Seeds

Seeds of *Rosa polyantha nana*, offered as "baby roses," are available from several seedsmen. If you sow seeds in spring, you will have plants in bloom two to three months after germination. First condition seeds by placing them in half an inch of water in a refrigerator dish, and put this in a freezer. Last year I put seeds into the freezing unit on April 23. On May 15 I removed the dish, melted the ice, and planted the seeds in a mixture of peat moss and sand. By May 29 there were several sets of true leaves, and the plants came into full bloom the last of June (in spite of the small neighbor boy who transplanted them, mostly tops *down* when we were out of town for five days). The seeds produced neat little bushes, 5 to 12 inches high, and fragrant single and semi-double flowers in shades of pink and white.

Like other miniature roses, these tiny polyanthas are hardy and may be planted outdoors around the year, or brought inside for the winter. However, I do not think these are as lovely for a window garden or home greenhouse as are the named varieties of the hybrid-tea type.

ILLUSTRATION 57. *'Sheri Anne' has 1½-inch flowers of red-orange. Photograph courtesy Ralph Moore.*

🌿 Ways To Use

Miniature roses indoors can be enjoyed in various ways. Grow them individually in pots, or set a row of them in a brass or copper planter or redwood window box that fits a sunny window sill. (For best results, leave plants in pots and sink them to the rims in moist peat moss.) Turn the planter every few days so that the plants will have equal light on all sides. In the greenhouse, grow them in a strawberry jar, or devote a bench to a garden of bush, climbing and tree miniature roses. Hanging baskets of bush or climbing varieties are great to grow in a home greenhouse or cool sun porch in the winter. When warm weather arrives, clip back old growth and put outdoors for the summer; just be sure that miniature roses in a hanging basket never dry out severely. Cut the flowers freely for arrangements, for boutonnieres, or even for decorating a cake. For a dinner party, put a tiny bud vase with a miniature rose in it at each place setting.

The leading breeders of miniature roses are Ralph Moore of Visalia, California, Ernest Williams of Dallas, Texas, the House of Meilland (the French originators of 'Peace,' the most famous rose of all time) and Pedro Dot, a Spanish

ILLUSTRATION 58. *Miniature roses grow beautifully in a ceramic strawberry jar. Photograph courtesy Star Roses.*

breeder, whose new varieties, like those of Meilland, are introduced in this country by Star Roses, West Grove, Pennsylvania. Once you grow a few miniature roses, you will like them so much, you will watch magazines and catalogs for announcements of new varieties.

ILLUSTRATION 59. *Miniature tree rose and bush miniature. (Scale: bush in 3-inch pot.) Photograph courtesy Star Roses.*

11. A Multitude of Excellent Miniature Plants

There are hundreds—even thousands—of miniature plants that mature at less than 10 inches, most of them below 6. Many of these are described in this chapter, along with a few notes on the way they grow—leaf formation and coloring, flowers and fruits. The season of bloom for the hardy perennial alpine plants may be several weeks earlier inside a cool greenhouse or cold frame; the dates given are for the natural outdoor flowering times. The code to culture is keyed by numbers to the chart that begins at the end of this chapter.

The culture of some of these miniatures is delightfully easy, and such plants are marked by an asterisk (*). The majority of them are easy if their few cultural requirements are met. Seeds and plants of most of them are available in this country. (Sources are given at the back of the book.) Do keep each plant labeled for its own sake and to add to your knowledge and pleasure. Include on the label, with the name of the plant, the date you received it, from whom and any other information you consider pertinent. Records like this are invaluable.

🐿 MINIATURES FROM ACAENA TO WAHLENBERGIA

(*Abbreviations:* DT = dwarf tree; Fls = flowers; HA = hardy annual; HHA = half-hardy annual; HP = hardy perennial; HHP = half-hardy perennial; HS = hardy shrublet; Lvs = leaves; TH = tender or tropical herb; TC = tender cactus; TS = tender succulent.)

ACAENA (uh SEE nuh). Rosaceae. *A. buchananii,* HP, 2″, trailing, silver-green lvs. and red burrs in summer. S. Island, New Zealand. *microphylla,* HP, 2″, mat-forming, bronzy evergreen lvs. and red, spiny fls. in summer; var *inermis,* 2″, the same with spineless fls. Culture: 4 or 6; 9 in winter; 13; 16 or 17; 24 or 26. Propagation: 31 or 32, 34 in late summer, or 36 spring or fall. Uses: 38, 39, 41, or 42 (large shallow pot to allow trailing room).

ACANTHOPHYLLUM (uh kanth o FYE lum). Caryophyllaceae. *A. spinosum,* HP, 3″, tufting, prickly lvs. Fragrant, rose-pink fls. July-Sept. Culture: 6; 9; 13; 16; 24. Propagation: 32, or 36 in early spring. Uses: 39, 41, or 42.

ACER (AY sir). Aceraceae. *A. palmatum dissectum,* DT. Bronze-crimson deeply cut leaves, 7- to 11-lobed; scarlet in fall. Begin with a young, container-grown seedling. Prune and train as a miniature tree. Culture: 5, 6, or 7; 9-10; 13; 15, 16, or 17; 22. Uses: 39, 41, 42, or bonsai.

ACHILLEA (ak uh LEE uh). Compositae. *A. ageratifolia,* HP, 4″, compact mounds of silver foliage; pure white fls. in summer. *tomentosa,* HP, 6″, wooly lvs. and sunny yellow fls. June to Sept. *umbellata,* HP, 4″, mounds of silver lvs., and white fls. June to Sept. Culture: 6; 9 in winter; 13; 19 in winter; 21. Propagation: 36 in the spring. Uses: 39, 41, or 42.

* ACHIMENES (ak KIM in eez). Gesneriaceae. All hybrids and cultivars available in commerce of this tender herb are desirable. Under conventional culture a half dozen or more of the scaly rhizomes are planted in a hanging basket or large pot. To grow a smaller plant, use one or two of the

catkin-like rhizomes in a 3- or 4″ pot. Pinch growing tips frequently until middle of June. The resulting plant will be a small bush, semi-upright or trailing, under 10″ overall. Tropical America. Culture: 3, 4, 5, 6, 7, or 8; 11; 13 after planting in spring until growth begins, then 14, but nearly dry during dormancy in late fall and winter; 16-17; 22, 24, 25, 27, 28, or 29. Propagation: 32, 34 (the scaly rhizomes multiply rapidly). Uses: 38 or 42.

* ACORUS (AK or us). Araceae. *A. gramineus pusillus*, HP, 2–3″, tufts of iris-like lvs. *gramineus variegatus*, HP, 6–9″, forms clumps of green- and white-striped iris-like fans. Culture: 3, 4, 5, 6 or 7; 10–11; 15–16; 26. Propagation: 36 in the spring. Uses: 37, 39, 40, or 41 for *gramineus pusillus* (Illustration 60); 38, 40, or 42 for *gramineus variegatus*.

ADIANTUM (ad ee AN tum). Polypodiaceae. *A. bellum*, Bermuda maidenhair fern, 6″, makes active growth in winter, rests in summer and during that time should be grown on dry side. *capillus-veneris*, (see Illustration 98) miniature maidenhair, 6″. *hispidulum*, similar to others, with dark green, branching fronds. Culture: 1, 2, or 8; 9–10; 13 Sept. to March, 14 balance of year, except as noted for *bellum;* 16–17; 22 with one part chipped charcoal or 29. Propagation: 36 in fall or spring. Uses: 38, 39, 40, or 42.

* ADROMISCHUS (ad ROH mish us). Crassulaceae. Miniature succulents, all exceedingly showy and desirable. Culture: 5, 6, or 7; 10; 12; 15–16; 21 or 24. Propagation: 33 or 36. Uses: 39a or 42.

ILLUSTRATION 60. Acorus gramineus pusillus.

* AFRICAN VIOLETS, Miniature, see Chapter 3.

AGERATUM (adge uhr AY tum). Compositae. *A. mexicanum*
'Little Blue Star,' HHA, 6", quilted leaves of bright green and
heads of sky blue fls. Try other dwarf varieties; if they prove
too tall for indoors, utilize them in the outdoor garden.
Culture: 5 or 6; 9 or 10 in winter; 13; 16; 26. Propagation:
33, preferably in Jan. or Aug. Uses: 39 or 42.

*AGLAONEMA (agg lo NEE muh). Araceae. *A. pictum*, TH, upright,
with blue-green leaf, dashingly splashed with silver; overall
iridescence. var. *tricolor* and other species *commutatum
albo-variegatum* and *treubii* are small while they are young.
Culture: 3, 4, 5, 6, 7, or 8; 10; 13–14; 16, 17, or 18; 24, 26, or 29.
Propagation: 36. Uses: 40 or 42.

AJUGA (uh JEW guh). Labiatae. *A. reptans variegata*, HP, 6",
stoloniferous, mat-forming with rosettes of green lvs. variegated with pale pink and cream: blue fls., May to July.
Culture: 6; 9–10; 13; 15–16; 22. Propagation: 32, or 36 in
early spring or autumn. Uses: 38 or 42.

*ALLOPHYTON (al loh FYE ton). Scrophulariaceae. A. *mexicanum*,
syn. Tetranema mexicanum, the Mexican foxglove, TH, 3"
tall, 4" in diameter. Rosettes of dark green leaves, glossy at
first, then smooth. Flowers intense reddish lavender and
white, similiar to those of *Sinningia pusilla* (see Chapter
2). Everblooming, eventually growing out of the pot as an
old African violet. When this happens, either start a new

ILLUSTRATION 61. Allophyton
mexicanum.

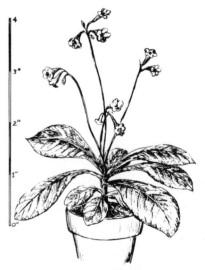

1. Miniature pink and blue African violets with miniature rex begonia, photographed with standard-size African violet to show scale.

2. David Cullen's large terrarium holds more than 100 miniatures (*Sinningia* species and cultivars). A glass cover assures constant high humidity.

3. Sinningia 'Wood Nymph' from the large terrarium shown above.

4. Plastic storage box provides a sweat-box home
for thriving selaginella miniatures, variegated creeping
fig, *Gesneria cuneifolia,* and miniature gloxinias.

5. Sinningia 'Cindy' from sweat box shown above.

6. A 14-inch square plastic Parson's table with recessed planter on top and clear cover nurtures a miniature landscape by David Cullen.

7. Detail of table terrarium shown above includes miniature oak-leaved creeping fig, orange-flowered gesneria, white sinningia and blue African violet.

8. From left to right, miniature geranium, miniature African violet and rooted cutting of honeysuckle fuchsia ('Gartenmeister Bohnstedt'), with thimble for scale.

9. Living stones or lithops, with quarter for scale. From the collection of David Cullen.

10. Miniature selaginella or sweat plant in 2¼-inch pot.

11. Variegated strawberry-geranium, *Saxifraga stolonifera* 'Tricolor.'

12. 'Pixie Blue' miniature African violet, with lemon for scale.

13. Miniature sinningia hybrid from the collection of Mrs. Philip Sarna, photographed in eggshell for scale.

plant from seeds, lower the old plant in the pot, adding new soil, or cut it off and root the top part of the rosette. Culture: 3, 4, 5, 6, 7, or 8; 10; 13–14; 16, 17, or 18; 24, 26, or 29. Propagation: 33 or 36. Uses: 39, 40, or 42. (Illustration 61.)

*ALOE (uh LOW ee). Liliaceae. *A. variegata*, to 12″ when in flower. Lvs. strikingly striped transversely; fls. of reddish pink are densely set on the spike, thus providing a showy display for about a month. There are many other species of aloe that are useful as miniatures, some permanently, others while they are in the juvenile state. Culture: 5, 6, or 7; 9–10; 13 in late spring to Aug., then 12; 15; 21. Propagation: 33. Uses: 39a or 42.

*ALTERNANTHERA (alter NANTH er uh). Amaranthaceae. *A. bettzickiana*, TH, 3–4″,. forms a dense mound of small lvs. variegated with yellow, pink, and maroon on green; var. *aurea nana* has green and gold lvs. *versicolor* has small maroon-green leaves splashed with rose-pink or cream. These plants are known popularly as joseph's-coat. Pinching back may be necessary to encourage compactness. Culture: 5, 6, 7, or 8; 10; 13; 15–16; 22, 24, or 26. Propagation: 34. Uses: 39, 40, or 42.

ALYSSUM (uh LISS um). Cruciferae. *A. montanum*, HP, 2–4″, tuft-forming gray-green lvs., and bright yellow, fragrant fls. May-July. Culture: 6; 9–10; 13; 15–16; 22 or 26. Propagation: 31 or 32, 34.

ALYSSUM, SWEET, see under Lobularia.

ANACAMPSEROS (anna CAMP sir us). Portulacaceae. *A. budieriana*, and many other miniature succulents of this genus. At a glance they appear to be slender pine cones. Culture: 5, 6, or 7; 9–10 in winter; 12 fall and winter, 13 spring and summer; 15; 20 with some old mortar and chipped brick. Propagation: 32, or 34 any time. Uses: 39a or 42.

ANACYCLUS (anna SIKE lus). Compositae. *A. depressus*, HP, 2″, trailing with white daisy fls., the petals tipped with crimson, and appearing in the summer. Morocco. Revels in sunlight. Culture: as for Achillea.

ANDROMEDA (an DRAHM ih duh). Ericaceae. *A. polifolia glaucophylla*, dwarf shrublet with narrow gray lvs. and pink fls.;

polifolia grandiflora is a beautiful Japanese species of dwarf growth, glaucous lvs., and large pink bell flowers; *polifolia minima* forms a miniature shrublet with large pink flowers in earliest spring. Culture: 6; 9 in winter, 13; 16–17; 25 with half by volume of acid peat moss. Propagation: by layering in early fall. Uses: 39, 41, or 42.

ANDROSACE (an DROSS uh cee). Primulaceae. *A. carnea*, HP, 2″, rosettes of smooth, green lvs., with yellow-eyed pink fls. in the spring; var. *brigantica*, 2–4″, forms a neat tuft of narrow green lvs., and sends small umbels of white, tinted pink, fls. in March and April. *helvetica*, 1″, has pink flowers that fade to white from June to July (Illustration 62); *imbricata*, 2″, is covered with stemless white fls. in the spring. *lanuginosa leichtlinii*, 4″, is a creeping or trailing plant with silver lvs. and pink- or yellow-eyed white fls. from May to Sept. *pyrenaica*, 2″, has gray-green hummocks of foliage with a profusion of stemless white fls. in May or June. *sarmentosa*, 4″, has rosettes of silver-haired lvs. that spread by stolons, and soft pink heads of fls. May to June; var. *chumbyi*, 4–6″, has silvery, downy lvs. and bright pink fls., April-May; var. *watkinsii* (syn. *A. limprichtii*), 4–5″, has large green rosettes with soft pink to rose-red fls. May-June, *sempervivoides*, 2″, has incurved lvs. that form tiny rosettes and crimson-eyed pink fls. in April or May. Culture: 6, 9; 12; 19; 23 with a sprinkling of bone meal. Propagation: 30, or 34 or 36 in the spring. Uses: 41 or 42.

ANEMONE (uh NEM oh nee). Ranunculaceae. *A. blanda rosea*, HP, 6″, has deeply cut lvs. and pink fls. early in the spring. *nemerosa alleni*, HP, 6″, fls. freely from April to June with blooms of glistening lavender-blue. Both of these will bloom in March in a cool greenhouse. Culture: 6; 9; 13; 15–16; 24 with one part well-rotted cow manure. Propagation: 31, or 34 in the spring. Uses: 39, 41 or 42.

ANTHYLLIS (an THYE liss). Leguminosae.. *A. hermanniae*, HS, 10″ spiny shrublet covered with orange-yellow fls. June-July. *montana rubra*, 3″, forms dense, ground-hugging mats of lvs. and in May-June sends up its crimson, clover-like fls. Culture: 6; 9; 13; 16; 24. Propagation: 34 in Aug. Uses: 39, 41, or 42.

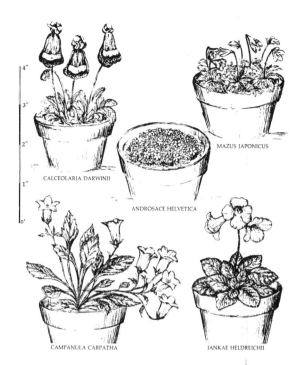

CALCEOLARIA DARWINII

MAZUS JAPONICUS

ANDROSACE HELVETICA

CAMPANULA CARPATHA

JANKAE HELDREICHII

ILLUSTRATION 62. *Collection of miniature alpine plants.*

ANTIRRHINUM (anter RYE num). Scrophulariaceae. Dwarf or miniature snapdragons. *A. asarina,* HHP, 6″, has trailing cordate lvs., and large fls. of pale yellow. *glutinosum,* HP, 2″, has ground-hugging blue-green lvs., and yellow-white fls., the lip of each striped with red, in July. *nanum compactum* Sutton's Little Gem hybrids, HHA, 4–6″, compact plants completely covered with wee snapdragon fls. in unusual and pleasing colors. Culture: 5, 6; 10–11; 12–13; 15–16; 24. Propagation: 32. Uses: 38 for *Asarina,* 39, 41, and 42 for others.

ARABIS (AIR uh biss). Cruciferae. *A. androsacea,* HP, 1″, has white fls. May-June. *blepharophylla,* 3–6″, has fls. of intense carmine which appear in Jan. in a cool frame or a greenhouse. *bryoides olympica,* 1″, has tufts of silver foliage and white fls. in spring. *rosabella,* 4″, is a compact plant with bright pink fls. in spring. *sturii,* 2–3″, forms cushions of dark, glossy lvs., and has white fls.; may be flowered in mid-winter in a cool frame or a greenhouse. Culture: 6, 9; 12–13; 15–16 except 19 for *androsacea* and *bryoides olympica;* 21, 22 or 24. Propagation: 32, 34 in Aug. 36 in Oct. Uses: 41 or 42.

*ARALIA (uh RAY lee uh). Araliaceae. *A. fruticosa* 'Parsley,' TH, may be grown as a compact miniature tree of lacy, cut lvs. Culture: 3, 4, 5, or 6; 10; 13; 16; 22, 26, or 29. Uses: 39 or 42. Now more properly called *polyscias fruticosa.*

ARCTERICA (arc TARE ih kuh). Ericaceae. *A. nana,* HP, 3–4", a cushion evergreen that bears fragrant, white fls. spring and fall. At a glance they appear to be lily-of-the-valley fls. Culture: 4 or 6; 9 in the winter; 13; 16; 24 with the addition of three parts acid peat moss. Uses: 39, 41, or 42.

ARENARIA (are NAY ree uh). Caryophyllaceae. *A. balearica,* HP, ½", a miniature at the vanishing point with minute creeping stems, set with light green lvs., and sparked with small white fls. May to July, *purpurascens,* HP, 1", has cushions of green lvs., and lavender-pink fls. in spring. *tetraquetra,* 2–3", has unusual foliage, the lvs. being arranged in four rows; has heads of white fls. in summer. Culture: 6; 9 in winter; 13; 19 in winter; 21. Propagation: 32, or 36 in early spring. Uses: 39, 41 or 42.

ARMERIA (are MEER ee uh). Plumbaginaceae. *A. juniperifolia,* syn. *A. caespitosa,* HP, 2", evergreen-like lvs., and small heads of pale lilac fls. Culture: 6; 9; 12–13; 15–16; 21. Propagation: 32, 36 fall or spring. Uses: 41 or 42.

ASPERULA (as PAIR yew luh). Rubiaceae. *gussonei,* HP, 2–6", tuft-forming with dense, dark green lvs. and light pink fls. in the spring, *hirta,* HP, 2", pink and white fls. in the spring. *pontica,* 1", cushion of gray lvs., and light rose fls. May or June. *suberosa,* 2", tufts of silvery, wooly lvs., and rose-pink, trumpet-shaped fls. Culture: 6; 9; 13; 15–16; 22. Propagation: 31, 36 in March. Uses: 41 or 42.

ASPIDIUM. See Polystichum.

ASTILBE (as TILL bee). Saxifragaceae. *A. crispa* 'Gnom,' HP, 4–6", rosette of dwarf, crinkled lvs., and dark pink flowers in spikes. Aug.-Sept. *sinensis pumila,* 6–8", is similar, but fls. later and of lilac-purple. Culture: 6; 9; 14 when in active growth; 16; 22, substituting well-rotted cow manure for peat moss if possible. Pot early in the fall, store in a cold frame covered with peat moss or leaf mold until December. Then move to 45–50° for seven to ten days; then 55–60°. Apply organic fertilizer such as fish emulsion when buds show. Put outdoors in summer, repot in the fall. Propagation: 36 in early summer. Uses: 39, 41, or 42.

*ASTROPHYTUM (as troh FYE tum). Cactaceae. *A. myriostigma* is a dark green, five-ribbed body heavily and uniformly dotted with white. Even young plants bloom, with fls. of vivid, glistening yellow. Most species of astrophytum are valuable for 39a or 42. Culture: 3, 4, 5, 6, or 7; 10–11; 12; 15–16; 20 or 21. Propagation: 33. Uses: 39a or 42.

AZALEA, see *Rhododendron.*

BABIANA (babby AY nuh). Iridaceae. *B. stricta rubrocyanea,* HHP, 6–8″, a bulbous plant with red-throated fls. of intense deep blue in May. Plant the corms in August or September, 1″ deep, 12 to a 6-inch pot, or 1 to a 3-inch container. Culture: 5 or 6; 9–10; 14, except dry during summer; 16–17; 20 with a teaspoon of bone meal added to each 6-inch pot. Uses: 42.

*BAMBUSA (bam BOO zuh). Gramineae. *B. nana,* the dwarf bamboo. (Botanists may refer to this species as either *B. glaucescens* or *B. multiplex.*) Prune it as necessary to keep at desired size and shape. Culture: 3, 4, 5, 6, or 7; 10–11; 13–14; 15, 16 or 17; 22, 27, or 29. Propagation: 36. Uses: 39, 40, or 42.

BEGONIAS, Miniature or Small-growing, see Chapter 4.

BELLIS (BELL iss). Compositae. *B. perennis* 'Dresden China,' HP, 2″, a dwarf daisy with double pink fls. in the spring; 'Rob Roy' is similar, but fls. are crimson and slightly larger. Culture: 4, 5, 6, or 8; 9; 13; 16; 24. Propagation: 31, 36 in June. Uses: 39, 41, or 42.

BELLIUM (BELL ee um). Compositae. *B. minutum,* HA, 2–3″, miniature daisy, the rays of the fls. white, purplish pink on the reverse, and the disk yellow. Culture: 5 or 6; 9; 13; 15–16; 21. Propagation: 31. Uses: 39, 41, or 42.

BERBERIS (BER ber iss). Berberidaceae. *B. candidula,* HS, forms a low, rounded bush that may be kept under 12 inches by careful pruning; has bright yellow fls., purple fruits. Culture: 6; 10; 12; 16; 21. Uses: 39, 41, or 42.

*BERTOLONIA (ber toh LOH nee uh). Melastomaceae. *B. maculata* (see Illustration 63), TH, has puckered, elliptic lvs. of maroon-green above, intense rose-red beneath, and they are marked on the top by a slender stripe of silver down the midrib. *marmorata*, TH, is useful as a miniature while it is young. It has handsome, quilted lvs. of velvety green with silver striping, rosy beneath, and lavender-purple fls. *pubescens* has puckered green lvs. that are broadly banded with purple-brown through the mid-section. Culture: 1, 2, 3, 4, 7, or 8; 10–11; 13–14; 16, 17 or 18; 22, 25, 27, 28, or 29. Propagation: 36. Uses: 40 or 42.

*BILLBERGIA (bill BERG ee uh). Bromeliaceae. *B. morelli*, 10″, a dwarf billbergia with blunt-tipped green lvs. and blue fls. sheathed in rosy red. Culture: 1, 2, 3, 4, 5, 6, 7, or 8; 10–11; 13; 16–17; 21, 22, or osmunda fiber. Uses: 39a, applying water to center of leaf rosette as often as it is absorbed in the air and by the plant, or 42.

* BRYOPHYLLUM (brye oh FYE lum). Crassulaceae. *B.* 'Houghton's' as offered in commerce. A miniature variety that gives the illusion of a wind-swept coconut palm. Culture: 5, 6, or 7; 10–11; 12–13; 15; 21. Propagation: 34. Uses: 39a or 42.

*CALADIUM (kuh LAY dee um). Araceae. *C. humboldtii*, syn. C. argyrites, TH, 9″, miniature lvs. of typical caladium shape, dark but vibrant green with clean-cut markings of white. One of the choicest miniature house plants. In overall size, there are no other caladiums as small as *humboldtii*. However there are numerous magnificent recent hybrids that are classified as dwarf and bushy. These include 'Bride's Blush,' 'Buck,' 'Candidum Jr.,' 'Coral Glow,' 'Debutante,' 'Kathleen,' 'Leather Neck,' 'Lord Derby,' 'Lord Rosenberry,' 'Miss Marveen,' 'Mrs. Arno Nehrling,' 'Pink Beauty,' 'Pink Radiance,' 'Poecile Angalis,' 'Red Ace,' 'Red Flash,' 'Red Polka,' 'Red Sail,' and 'Sea Gull.' Also, these strap- and lance-leaf varieties: 'Little Rascal,' 'O. E. Orpit,' 'Flame Beauty' and 'Miss Prissy.' Culture: 2, 3, 4, 5, 6, 7, or 8; 11; 13–14; 16–17; 22 or 24 with addition of one part well-rotted cow manure. Uses: 40 or 42.

*CALATHEA (kal uh THE uh). Marantaceae. *C. bachemiana*, TH, feather-shaped lvs. of gray-green with bold dashes along midrib, and a slender margin of dark, velvety green along the edges. *micans*, TH, 6″, oblong-lanceolate lvs. of iridescent green with well defined center marking of silver-white. *picturata argentea*, TH, 8″, short, broad, elliptic lvs. are silver with distinct edging of dark green. *picturata vandenheckei* has lvs. similar in shape to previous variety, but they are deep, nearly black-green, with center feathering of silver-white, and a slender line of silver about ¼ to ½ inch from the leaf edge running parallel on either side. *roseo-picta*, TH, 8″, has beautiful, variegated lvs. *undulata*, TH, 8″, has leaf of deep green with silver stripe down the midrib. *wiotii*, TH, 7″, has elliptic lvs. of bright, light green, with oblong circles of dark, velvety

ILLUSTRATION 63. *A window garden of miniature plants. Top row, left to right:* Oxalis hedysaroides rubra, Ludisia discolor *and* Glecoma hederacea variegata. *Middle row:* Bertolonia maculata *and* Saxifraga stolonifera tricolor. *Bottom row:* Chamaeranthemum igneum *and* Chamaeranthemum venosum. *Photograph by Kari Berggrav.*

green on either side of the midrib. Culture: 3, 4, or 8; 11; 14; 22 with addition of one part well-rotted cow manure, or 29. Propagation: 36. Uses: 40 or 42.

CALCEOLARIA (kal see oh LAY ree uh). Scrophulariaceae. *C. biflora*, HP, 5–6″, lvs. mat-forming, sending up slender stems June-July, each topped by twin flowers of brightest yellow. *darwinii*, HP, 3″, lvs. mat-forming, with amazing pouch fls. that are a combination of various shades of bronze, yellow and white. They appear in the summer. *fothergillii*, HP, 6″, yellow and red fls. May to Aug. *polyrrhiza*, HP, 6″, lvs. mat-forming and large, yellow fls. June to August, *tenella*, HP, 2″, creeping stems and yellow fls. June, the pouch of each marked with short, vertical dashes of reddish brown. Culture for all except *fothergillii:* 4 or 6; 9; 13; 16; 24, or 25 with addition of one part well-rotted cow manure. Propagation: 31, 36 in March. Uses: 39, 41, or 42. Culture for *fothergillii:* 4 or 6; 9—maximum night-time temperature Aug. to March is 50°, 55° March to May; 13 until in flower, then 14; 16 or 17; soil same as for other species. Propagation: sow seeds in July, and discard plants after they finish blooming. Uses: 39, 41, or 42.

CALLOPSIS (kal OPP sis). Araceae. *C. volkensii*, 2–4″, white spathe and yellow spadix in summer or fall. Culture: 2, 3, 4, or 8; 10–11; 16, 17, or 18; 22, 25, or 29. Propagation: 36. Uses: 40 or 42.

CALLUNA (kal LOO nuh). Ericaceae. *C.* var. *minima*, HP, minute variety with white fls. Aug. and Sept. 'Mullion' is a compact, ball-like plant to 6″ with deep pink fls. Culture: 4 or 6; 9; 12–13; 25 with addition of four parts acid peat moss. Propagation. 34 in Aug., rooted in peat moss and sand in high humidity, 36 Oct. or April. Uses: 41 or 42.

CAMPANULA (kam PAN yeu luh). Campanulaceae. *C. allionii*, HP, 3–6″, purple fls. in June. *arvatica*, HP, 2–3″, starry fls. of deep violet-blue; var. *alba* has white fls. *aucheri*, HP, 4″, huge fls. of satiny purple in June. *betulaefolia*, HP, 3″, pink fls. in May. *carpatha*, HP, 6″, pale lavender fls. in summer; *cochleariifolia*, syn. *pusilla*, HP, 3–4″, nodding bell flowers of pale blue, June-July. *elatines*, HP, 4″, starry fls. of purple, July-Sept.; var. *garganica hirsuta*, HP, 3–4″, has star-shaped fls. of bright blue, July-Aug.; var. *garganica* 'W. H. Paine,' HP, 4″, has summer fls. of intense blue with contrasting centers of white. *fenestrellata*, a form of *elatines*, HP, 3–4″, has starry fls. of china-blue, June-July. *fragilis*, HP, 4–6″, grows as a trailer with fls. of light lilac-blue in Aug. 'G. F. Wilson,' HP, 6″, lilac or violet, bell flowers in July. *glomerata acaulis*, HP, 3–6″, clusters of blue fls. June-Aug. *isophylla*, HHP, 4–6″, lilac-blue, silvery blue, white or mauve fls. depending on var., usually in summer and early fall; one of the most outstanding basket plants that may be grown in a cool to moderate sunny window. 'Miranda,' HP, 3″, silver-blue bell flowers in profusion from June to Sept. *petiolata*, HP, 6″, large bells of dark blue in the summer. *portenschlagiana*, syn *muralis*, HP, 4″, large blue fls. through most of the summer. 'Profusion,' HP, 4–5″, silver-blue bell flowers on erect stems during July and Aug. *pulla*, HP, 4″, attractive glossy lvs. with bells of satin-like violet on slender stems in June or July; it likes a lime soil. *raineri*, HP, 3″, has blue fls. in July; var. *alba* has white fls. 'R. B. Loder,' HP, 4″, has semi-double fls. of medium blue in Aug. *rotarvatica*, HP, 3″, an exceptional plant, completely dainty, and described by Hillier & Sons of England as a "dwarf harebell"; blooms July to Sept. *stansfieldii*, HP, 3–4″, has lavender-violet fls. June-Aug. *turbinata*, HP, 4″, has large, open blue bell fls. on short stems June-Aug. *warleyensis*, HP, 3″, is a gem of a plant with blue, double fls. in the summer. Culture: 5 or 6; 9; 13 in winter, 14 in summer; 16, 22 or 24. Propagation: sow seeds in Aug., 34, 36 in early spring. Uses: 39, 41, or 42; trailing varieties are choice for 38.

CAREX (CARE ex). Cyperaceae. *C. variegata*, HHP, described by Logees of Connecticut as a dwarf plant with grassy lvs. striped green and white. Culture: 4, 5, 6, 7; 9; 14; 15–16; 24. Propagation: 36 in March. Uses: 42.

CARISSA (kuh RISS uh). Apocynaceae. *C. grandiflora* 'Boxwood Beauty' tropical evergreen, a dwarf form of the Natal plum. Besides thick, glossy lvs. it has waxy, starry, and fragrant fls. of white. Culture: 1, 2, 3, 4, or 8; 10–11; 13, 15, 16 or 17; 22, 26, or 29. Propagation: 34 of half-matured wood. Uses: 39 or 42. Shape and prune the plant as desired.

CASSIOPE (kuh SIGH oh pee). Ericaceae. *C. lycopodioides*, hardy evergreen, mat-forming shrub, 2–3″, with beautiful white fls. in the spring. Difficult. Culture: 2 or 4; 9; 13–14; 16; 23 with the addition of three parts peat moss. Propagation: 30, 34, or by layering. Uses: 41a or 42.

CELOSIA (suh LOH see uh). Amaranthaceae. *C.* Dwarf Pygmy, or Dwarf Florists Strain, TH, less than 6″, with a ruff of green leaves almost at ground level, and fist-size flower heads of glowing, pastel colors. Annuals to be discarded after the flowers begin to lose their color. Culture: 6; 10–11; 13; 16; 26 with addition of one part well-rotted cow manure. Propagation: 32. Uses: 42.

CELSIA (SELL see uh). Scrophulariaceae. *C. acaulis*. HP, 2″, with rosettes of crinkled or quilted lvs. and yellow fls. with stamens of glowing orange. Culture: 6; 9 in winter; 13; 16–17; 24 or 26 with the addition of a half part well-rotted cow manure. Propagation: 31 or 32, or 34. Uses: 41 or 42.

CENTAURIUM (sen TAR ee um). Gentianaceae. *C. chloodes*, 3″, is a mound-forming alpine with fls. of bright pink in summer or early fall. They are shaped like a gentian. Culture: 6; 9 in winter; 13; 16–17; 21 with the addition of three parts peat moss. Propagation: 31, or 36 in early spring. Uses: 41 or 42.

*CEROPEGIA (seer oh PEE gee uh). Asclepiadaceae. *C. barkleyi*, TH, trailing or creeping with ovate lvs. of silver-gray, handsomely veined with pewter. *caffrorum*, TH, creeping or trailing with plain lvs. of dark green, the undersides sometimes suffused with rose. *debilis*, TH, creeping or trailing with rosy-backed green lvs. so slender they must be observed closely to be appreciated. *woodii*, TH, creeping or trailing with heart-shaped leaves of olive-green, evenly patterned with silver. These ceropegias bear almost grotesque, inch-long tubular fls. that are indescribable but attractive in a curious way. Culture: 3, 4, 5, 6, or 7; 9, 10 or 11; 12–13; 15 to 17; 24 or 26. Propagate by planting the bead-like bulbs that form along the stems. Uses: 38 or 42. Clip and train to keep to desired size.

CHAENOSTOMA (shay NOS toh muh). Scrophulariaceae. *C. fasti-giatum*, HA, 8″, fragrant, much-branched lvs. and stems, covered summer and fall with starry fls. of pink, or white in var. *alba.* Culture: 5 or 6; 9–10; 13 in winter, 14 in summer; 16; 26 with teaspoon of bone meal to each pot of soil. Propagation: 32. Uses: 38 or 42.

*CHAMAERANTHEMUM (shay muh RANTH ee mum). *C. gaudichaudii,* TH, creeping, 3–6", ovate lvs. of dark green, with a broad midrib marking of silver that feathers out along each vein. *igneum,* TH, 6–9", has slender lvs. of velvety bronze-brown with glowing veins of pinkish gold; often classified as *Stenandrium igneum. venosum,* TH, 3–6", similar to *gaudichaudii* except the silver markings are finer, giving the overall impression of a dark green leaf with silver veins rather than a silver leaf with variegation of green. Culture: 3, 4, 5, 6, 7, or 8; 10–11; 13-14; 16, 17 or 18; 22 or 29. Propagation: 34. Uses: 38, 40, 42.

CHIASTOPHYLLUM (key as toh FYE lum). Crassulaceae. *C. oppositofolium,* hardy succulent, 6", with lvs. similar to a 'Tom Thumb' kalanchoe, and graceful arching sprays of yellow fls. in summer. Treat as a sedum, which see.

*CHLOROPHYTUM (klor oh FYE tum). Liliaceae. *C. bichetii,* TH, 3–4", forms a tuft of green lvs. that are white-striped. Grows upright and does not produce the stolons produced by other species of chlorophytum which we know commonly as spider plants. Culture: 3, 4, 6, 7, or 8; 10–11; 13–14; 15, 16, 17 or 18; 22, 26, or 29. Propagation: 36. Uses: 39, 40, or 42.

*CHRYSANTHEMUM (kris ANTH ee mum). Compositae. *C. multicaule,* HA, 4–8", a miniature chrysanthemum, beginning to bloom at 4 inches with one-inch single fls. of brightest yellow. Fls. spring, summer, and fall. Culture: 5 or 6; 9–10; 13; 15–16; 24 or 26. Propagation: 32 or 33. Uses: 39 or 42.

*CISSUS (SISS us). Vitaceae. *C. striata,* TH, trailing or bushy, semiupright foliage plants with lacy, five-lobed lvs. of reddish green. (Illustration 64.) Culture: 3, 4, 5, 6, 7, or 8; 10 or 11; 13; 15, 16, 17 or 18; 24, 27 or 29. Propagation: 34. Uses: 39 or 42.

COCKSCOMB, see under Celosia.

CODIAEUM (koh DEE um). Euphorbiaceae. *C. variegatum pictum* var. *punctatum aureum,* TH, bushy miniature plant that may

ILLUSTRATION 64. Cissus striata, *miniature grape ivy. (Scale: leaf 1½ inches across.)*

need pruning to keep it in bounds, but easily kept under 12 inches. Slender linear lvs. of bright green, spotted with golden yellow. Culture: 3, 4, 5, or 6; 10–11; 13; 16, 17 or 18; 22, 26, or 29. Propagation: 34. Uses: 39, 40, or 42.

*CODONANTHE (koh doh NANTH ee). Gesneriaceae. *C. carnosa* has only recently come into cultivation. Waxy leaves and lovely white flowers produced in profusion (Illustration 65). Culture: 3, 6, 8; 11; 14; 17; 29. Propagation: 33, 34. Uses: 38.

*COLEUS (KOH lee us). Labiatae. *C. rehneltianus* and its varieties. Vigorous-growing creepers with small, highly colored, and variegated lvs. For a diminutive plant, cultivate in a hanging basket, preferably not over 6 inches in diameter, and pinch the growing tips as necessary to create a compact bush; train the stems to cover the basket and thus form a decorative ball of foliage. Culture: 3, 4, 5, 6, 7, or 8; 10–11; 13–14; 15, 16, 17, or 18; 22, 26, or 29. Propagation: 34. Uses: 38 or 42.

COLUMNEA (koh LUM nee ah). Gesneriaceae. *C. hirta*, TH, trailing plant of dark green, hairy lvs. and orange-red fls. *microphylla*, TH, trailing stems with close-set, small fuzzy opposite lvs. and fiery orange-red fls. New hybrids bred at Cornell, also by Michael Kartuz and others, are superb. Culture: 3, 4, 5, 6, 7, or 8; 10–11; 13; 15, 16 or 17; 22, 24, 25, 27, 28, or 29. Propagation: 34. Uses: 38, 40, or 42.

CONANDRON (koh NAN dron). Gesneriaceae. *C. ramondioides*, HP, 4–6″, with rosettes of hairy, quilted lvs. and lilac and

ILLUSTRATION 65.
Codonanthe carnosa.
(Scale: 3-inch pot.)

yellow fls. in the spring. Culture: 2 or 4; 9; 13; 19 in winter,
otherwise 16; 25. Propagation: 31, 36 in March. Uses: 41a
or 42.

CONOPHYTUM (koh noh FYE tum). Aizoaceae. *C. stephanii*, TS,
1″, very hairy pebble-like plants less than ¼-inch in diameter. *C. truncatellum*, TS, 4″, is a stone-like plant with
yellow fls. Aug.- Oct. Also, many other miniature species of
conophytum. Culture: 5, 6, or 7; 10; 13 Aug. and Sept., 12
balance of year; 15, 20 with addition of some mortar rubble
and brick dust. Propagation: 33. Uses: 37 or 42.

*CONVALLARIA (kon val LAY ree uh). Liliaceae. *C. majalis*, HP,
6–8″, lily-of-the-valley of gardens, may be forced into bloom
indoors in late winter or early spring, also vars. *rosea*, pink
fls., and *flora plena*, double white. Culture: 3, 4, 5, 6, 7, or 8;
9–10; 13–14; 15–16; 24, 27, 28, or 29. Propagation: 35. Uses:
42. If forced early at high temperatures, discard afterwards;
if flowered later, nearer normal blooming season, they may
be grown on in the outdoor garden through the summer,
ripened off in the fall, and forced again.

CONVOLVULUS (kon VOLV yeu lus). Convolvulaceae. *C. tenuis-
simus*, HP, 6″, forming a dense tuft of silver lvs. and bearing
large fls. of clear pink. Aug.-Sept. Culture: 6; 9 in the winter;
13; 19 in the winter, other times indifferent; 24 or 26.
Propagation: 32, 34, or 36 in early spring. Uses: 42.

COPTIS (KOP tiss). Ranunculaceae. *C. quinquefolia*, HP, 2–3″,
anemone-like lvs. and white fls. Feb.-March. Culture: 2 or 4;

9; 14; 16; 25 with addition of four parts peat moss. Propagation: 31, 36 Mar. or Oct. Uses: 41a or 42.

CORNUS (KOR nus). Cornaceae. *C. canadensis,* HS, 6–10″, the creeping dogwood, has carpets of foliage set in summer with starry, white fls., followed in the fall by glowing red berries. Culture: 6; 9 in winter; 13–14; 16–17; 25 with the addition of one part more of sand and four parts peat moss. Propagation: 34 or by layering. Uses: 41 or 42.

CORYDALIS (kor RID uh liss). Fumariaceae. *C. allenii,* HP, 3–4″, much-divided lvs., white and pink fls. in spring. *Halleri,* syn. *solida,* HP, 6″, bears spikes of purple fls. in April. Culture: 6; 9 in winter; 13; 16; 24 or 26. Propagation: 31 or 35. Uses: 41 or 42.

ILLUSTRATION 67. Crassula teres, *a miniature succulent.*

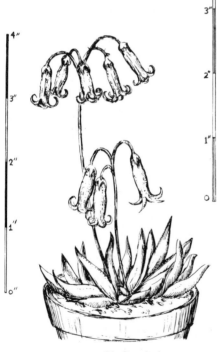

ILLUSTRATION 66. Cotyledon teretifolia, *a miniature succulent.*

*COTYLEDON (koh till EE dun). Crassulaceae. *C. chrysantha,* TS, 3", with rosettes of small, velvety lvs. and cream-yellow fls. July-Aug. *simplicifolia,* TS, 5–6", with arching, graceful sprays of tubular yellow fls. May to Aug. *teretifolia,* TS, 4–6", yellow, inverted bell flowers in summer. Culture: 5, 6, or 7; 11; 12; 15; 21. Propagation: 36 in March. Uses: 39a or 42. (Illustration 66).

*CRASSULA (KRASS yeu luh). Crassulaceae. *C. cooperi,* TS, 2–3", mat-forming lvs. of light green, dark, reddish depressed dots above, red on the undersides, and panicles of pale pink fls. *deceptrix,* TS, low, slow-growing handsome succulent of gray-white with white fls. 'Dregeana Hybrids,' TS, 4–6", thick-leaved rosettes bear central umbels of pink or crimson fls. over a period of several weeks. *falcata,* TS, 6", has yellow and red fls. in the summer. *schmidtii,* TS, dwarf rosettes of red-tinted lvs. with bright rose-pink fls. in the fall. *sediformis,* TS, 1", grows in dense rosettes of blue-green lvs. that turn to bronze and crimson-red in the fall. *teres,* TS, 2–4", the rattlesnake crassula (Illustration 67), forms small clusters of braid-like, white-edged, dark green lvs. and heads of fragrant, white fls. 'Triebneri Hybrid,' TS, small rosettes of pale green lvs. eye-lashed along the edges with tiny white hairs and stalks of pink fls., even on young plants; sold as the pink St. Andrew's cross and said to do well in rich, humusy soil. (Illustration 68.) Many pages could be devoted

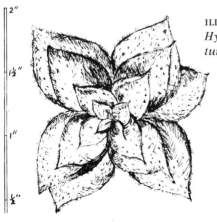

2"

1½"

1"

½"

ILLUSTRATION 68. '*Triebneri Hybrid*' crassula, a miniature succulent.

to still other species of crassula suitable for miniature gardens. In fact, it would be a fascinating, highly specialized hobby to collect just the varied species of this genus. Culture: 5, 6, or 7; 11 spring and summer, 10 fall and winter; 12 winter, 14 spring and summer, 13 in the fall; 15–16; 21 with addition of one part each of dried cow manure and brick rubble. Propagation: 32, 34 in the summer. Uses: 39 or 42.

*CROSSANDRA (cros AN druh). Acanthaceae. *C. infundibuliformis*, syn. C. undulaefolia, TH, 8–10″, with bright, glossy lvs. and bright, apricot- or salmon-orange fls. through most of the year. Culture: 3, 4, 5, 6, 7, or 8; 10–11; 13 in the winter, 14 spring to fall; 16–17; 22, 24, or 29. Propagation: 33 as soon as they are ripe, or 34. Uses: 42.

CROTON, miniature, see under Codiaeum.

*CRYPTANTHUS (kryp TANTH us). Bromeliaceae. *C. acaulis*, TH, rosettes of tough lvs. (like those of the pineapple), bronze-green and covered with beige speckling (Illustration 69). *bahianus*, TH, rosettes of recurved, wavy-edged lvs., dark red in color. *beucherii*, TH, rosettes of pale green lvs., marbled with a darker shade of green, and flat, spoon-shaped in formation; frequently sends up red and white fls. in the summer. *bivittatus*, or *roseus pictus*, TH, with rosettes of bronze-pink lvs., striped with pale green; white fls. in summer. *bromeloides tricolor*, TH, rosettes of green, handsomely variegated with ivory-white and suffused with rose-

ILLUSTRATION 69. Cryptanthus acaulis, *a miniature bromeliad.*

pink; tends to be more upright in growth than the others *terminalis*, TH, erect-growing rosettes of bronze-tinted, green lvs. *zonatus zebrina*, TH, rosettes of tan-striped, brownish green recurving lvs. cross-banded with chocolate stripes; may send up white fls. in the summer. Culture: 3, 4, 5, 6, 7, or 8; 10; 13 except less in fall and early winter; 15, 16, or 17; 24 combined with three parts osmunda fiber. Propagation, 36, removing the rosettes that form near the older plant. Uses: 39a, 42, or in the pockets of a small strawberry jar.

*CUPHEA (CUE fee uh). Lythraceae. *C. hyssopifolia*, tender shrub, 5–7″ in a 3-inch pot. Fine-leaved shrublet with lavender-pink fls. over a long period. Culture: 5 or 6; 10; 13 in winter, 14 in summer; 16; 22. Propagation: 32, 34. Uses: 42.

* CYANOTIS (sigh uh NOH tiss). Commelinaceae. *C. somaliensis*, TH, trailing plant with hairy stems and leaves, sometimes resulting in the plants being called pussy toes or pussy ears. Besides the unusual lvs., the plants have fls. of blue or light purple. Culture: 5, 6, or 7; 10–11; 12–13; 15–16; 24 or 26. Propagation: 34. Uses: 38, 39, 39a, or 42.

CYCLAMEN (SICK or SIKE luh men). Primulaceae. *C. coum*, HP, 4″, dark green, round lvs. and red fls. Feb.-Mar. *graecum*, HP, 3″, dark green lvs. with white veins, and rose-red fls. in the fall. *ibericum*, HP, 3″, beautiful round lvs., dark green with silver zone in pattern similar to choice zonale geraniums; red fls. Feb.-March. *neapolitanum*, HP, 3–4″, handsome

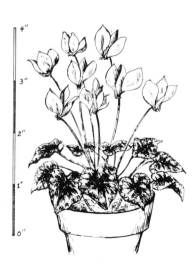

ILLUSTRATION 70. Cyclamen neapolitanum.

dark green lvs. with silver markings and summer or autumn
fls. of bright rose, marked with intense carmine blotch at
base (Illustration 70); available also in vars. *album*, white,
and *roseum*, rose. *repandum*, HP, 4″, silver-green lvs. shaped
similarly to those of the heuchera of outdoor gardens, and
rose-red fls. March-May. Culture: 4, 5, 6 or 8; 9 in winter; 13;
16–17; 22. Propagation: 30 or 35. Uses: 39, 41 or 42.

*CYPERUS (sigh PEER us). Cyperaceae. *C. elegans*, TH, 10–12″,
stoloniferous root sprouts send up umbrella-like lvs. of bright
green. Culture: 1, 2, 3, 4, or 8; 13 winter, 14 other times; 15,
16, or 17; 26. Propagation: 32, 36 in the spring. Uses: 39 as
a tree-like plant or 42.

CYRTANTHUS (seer TANTH us). Amaryllidaceae. *C. flanaganii*,
greenhouse bulb, 9″, strap-like lvs. and four to seven yellow
trumpet fls. to each stem in June. *rhododactylus*, greenhouse
bulb, 5–6″, two lvs. appearing with the fls. purple at the
base of the bulb, and rose fls. in Feb. Culture: 5, 6, or 7; 10;
12 during dormancy, 14 other times; 16; 26. Propagation: 33
when seeds are ripe, or 36 during dormancy. Uses: 42. When
in growth, the pots may be submerged in a miniature garden,
but removed after flowering ceases.

DAPHNE (DAFF nee). Thymelaeaceae. *D. blagayana*, HS, 9–12″,
shrublet with fragrant, white fls. March and April. 'Leila
Haines,' HS, fully dwarf shrublet with small lvs. and fragrant
fls. in the spring. *striata*, HS, 9″, weak, nearly prostrate
shrub, difficult to grow, but rewarding the gardener's trouble
with terminal clusters of rose- or purple-pink fls. May-July.
The flower tubes are striped with pink. This species is
closely related to *D. cneorum* but not nearly as easily, or as
widely, cultivated. Culture: 4 or 6; 9; 13 in winter, 14 other
times; 16–17; 26 with addition of one part peat moss. Propagation: 34 or by layering. Uses: 41 or 42. Best placed outdoors in partial to full shade in the summer; pinch out tips
of young growth in June.

DIANTHUS (die ANTH us). Caryophyllaceae. *D. alpinus*, HP,
3″, short-stemmed, large rose fls. June-July. *glauca nana*,
HP, 2″, tiny tufts of glaucous lvs. with pink fls. in the summer. 'Mars,' HP, 3″, a miniature with double, red fls. in the

summer. *microlepsis,* HP, 1″, rose-lilac fls. June or July; culture for this species as for others, except in soil mixture 23 with the addition of one part garden soil. *peristeria,* HP, 1″, mat-forming plant with small fls. of pink most of the summer. *roysii,* HP, 3″, a hybrid of *D. neglectus,* with fls. of vivid bright pink through most of the summer. *subacaulis,* HP, 1″, gray-leaved tiny plant with bright carmine flowers June and July. There are many other species and varieties of dianthus suitable for the cool or cold greenhouse, sun-heated pit, or cold frame. Culture: 6 (best in cold frame from fall to Feb.); 9; 13; 16; 26 with addition of one part well-rotted cow manure. Propagation: 32. Uses: 39, 41, or 42.

DIONAEA (die OH nee uh). Droseraceae (Carnivorous Plants). *D. muscipula* (see Illustration 71), HP, 4–6″, Venus fly trap. Rosettes of bright green leaves. Each leaf folds in the middle, the teeth along the edges interlocking to trap and hold insects; white fls. July and Aug. Best cultivated as a greenhouse perennial, or in a window garden if planted in a miniature greenhouse. Culture: 5, 6 or 8; 9; 14; 18; 25 with addition of four parts sphagnum moss. Propagation: 36. Uses: 40 or 42.

ILLUSTRATION 71. Dionaéa muscipula, *Venus flytrap. Photograph courtesy W. Atlee Burpee Company.*

DRABA (DRAY buh). Cruciferae. *D. aizoides,* HP, 3″, yellow fls. in March. *mollissima,* HP, 3″, mat-forming with blooms in the spring. *olympica,* HP, 3″, golden fls. in the spring. Culture: 6; 9; 12–13; 15–16; 24. Propagation: 31 or 32, 36 in March. Uses: 39, 41, or 42.

*DRACAENA (druh SEE nuh). Liliaceae. *D. godesffiana* 'Florida Beauty,' TH, under 10″ indefinitely. Tough green lvs. with creamy white spots, or sometimes almost creamy white leaves with a few green patches. Extremely slow growing, sometimes producing no new growth in several months, but the old foliage remains bright without any indication of withering or turning brown. Culture: 1, 2, 3, 4, 5, 6, 7, or 8; 10–11; 13–14; 15, 16, or 17; 26 or 29. Propagation: 34 in the spring. Uses: 39, 40, or 42.

DRYAS (DRY us). Rosaceae. *D. drummondii,* HP, 3″, yellow fls. in June. *suendermanii,* HP, 3–4″, is a slender-stemmed plant with elm-like lvs. and large white fls. with eight or more plump petals in June. Culture: 6; 9 in winter; 13–14; 16–17; plant in mixture of peat moss and sand. Propagation: 31 or 32, or 36 in spring or fall. Uses: 39, 41, or 42.

*ECHEVERIA (esch uh VEER ee uh). Crassulaceae. *E. derenbergii,* TS, known popularly as the painted lady. Rosettes of succulent, white-green lvs. margined with red. Fls. in the winter and spring even in a small pot. *setosa,* TS, hairy rosette with a succulent flower stem. Culture: 5, 6, or 7; 10–11; 13–14

ILLUSTRATION 72. *Episcia 'Pink Brocade' (sometimes called Cleopatra') has pink, cream-white and green leaves. It thrives in warmth and high humidity in a fluorescent-lighted garden. (Scale: leaf 1 inch long.)*

spring and summer, 12 other times; 15–16; 21. Propagation: 32, 34 in early fall. Uses: 39a or 42.

*ECHINOPSIS (eck in OPP sis). Cactaceae. *E. eyriessii*, TC, 4–6", white fls. in summer. *grandiflora*, TC, bears 5-inch fls. of rose-pink on plants less than 3 inches in diameter—among the easiest of all cacti to grow. Culture: 5, 6, or 7; 10–11; 12; 15; 21. Propagation: 32, 34 in summer. Uses: 39a or 42.

EDRAIANTHUS (ed rye ANTH us). Campanulaceae. *E. pumilio*, HP, 2–3", violet fls. in June. *serpyllifolius*, HP, 1", fls. in June of intense blue-purple coloring. *tenuifolius*, HP, 3–4", fine-cut lvs. and blue fls. in May. Culture: 6; 9 in winter; 12–13; 16; 21. Propagation: 31 or 32, or 36 in early spring. Uses: 39, 41, or 42.

*EPISCIA (eh PEE shuh). Gesneriaceae. *E. dianthiflora*, TH, trailing velvety leaves of bright but intense green, lightly veined with dark reddish brown; snow-white flowers lascin-iated as a dianthus, hence the species name, during the spring and summer, or any time the plant has good light, warmth, and high humidity. Hybrid episcias (Illustrations 72 and 73) are also highly desirable. Culture: 1, 2, 3, 4, or 8; 11; 13–14; 16, 17 or 18; 22, 25, 27, 28, or 29. Propagation: 32, 34 in spring or summer. Uses: 38.

ERICA (EH rih kuh). Ericaceae. *E. tetralix* var. 'Con Under-wood,' HS, 9", a dwarf heather, the best of those with deep crimson fls., blooms July-Sept. Culture: 6; 9; 13—uniformly

ILLUSTRATION 73. 'Silver Toy' *episcia*. (*Scale: 2½-inch pot.*)

moist at all times, preferably with rain water; 16; 25 with addition of four parts acid peat moss. Propagation: 34 in spring. Uses: 41 or 42. Prune new growth (shoots) drastically, even to 2 inches after flowering. Pot outdoors in partial sunlight in the summer, if possible.

ERINACEA (air in ACE ee uh). Leguminosae. *E. pungens*, HP, dwarf spiny bush, 8″, beautiful lavender-blue fls. May and June. Culture: 6; 9; 13; 16; 22. Propagation: 34 in cold frame in the fall. Uses: 42. Best put outdoors in the sun during the summer.

ERINUS (eh RYE nus). Scrophulariaceae. *E. alpinus*, HP, 4″, dwarf evergreen with red-purple fls. March to June; vars. 'Abbotswood Pink,' HP, 4″; *albus*, HP, 4″, white fls.; and 'Dr. Haenaele,' HP, 2″, and carmine fls. Culture: 6; 9; 12; 15–16; 24, preferably old mortar instead of sand. Propagation: 31, 36 in spring. Uses: 41 or 42.

ERYSIMUM (eh RISS ee mum). Cruciferae. *E. rupestre*, HP, 3″, tuft-forming miniature wallflower with yellow fls. in the spring. Culture: 6; 9 in winter; 13; 16–17; 24 or 26. Propagation: 31 or 32, 34 or 36 in early spring or fall. Uses: 39, 41, or 42.

*EUONYMUS (yew ON ee mus). Celastraceae. *E. japonicus microphyllus*, HP, to 10″ or more, but may be maintained at much less as a miniature hedge; bright green lvs. with pale yellow network of veins; var. *variegatus* is similar but has variegated lvs. (Illustration 74.) Culture: 3, 4, 5, 6, 7, or 8; 9–10; 13; 16, or 29. Propagation: 34. Uses: 39 or 42.

*EUPHORBIA (yew FOR bee uh). Euphorbiaceae. *E. splendens* var. 'Bojeri,' TS, described as a miniature form of the crown of thorns. In reality, it is just a smaller version—I have seen this variety grow to 3 feet in height. However, as a young rooted cutting, it is not difficult to prune and train the plant to under 12″. Wickedly thorny, but the small lvs. of bright green are fresh looking, and the bright red fls. in the winter and spring individually last for two weeks or more. Culture: 3, 4, 5, 6, 7 or 8; 10–11; 12; 15–16; 21, 24, or 26. Propagation: 34. Uses: 39a or 42.

EVERGREENS, miniature, dwarf and slow-growing, see Chapter 6.

ILLUSTRATION 74. Euonymus japonicus microphyllus *in a variegated form. (Scale: plant shown is 3 inches tall.)*

*EXACUM (EX uh kum). Gentianaceae. *E. affine,* tender biennial, 6–10″, small lvs. of bright green, sometimes lined with purple-black near the sinus, and starry blue-lilac, fragrant fls. from fall to spring, from a sowing of seeds made in March or April. Pinch back the seedlings when they are small to encourage compact, bushy growth. Culture: 5, 6, or 7; 10–11; 14; 16–17; 22. Propagation: 32. Uses: 42.

*FAUCARIA (foh KAY ree uh). Aizoaceae. *F. tigrina,* TS, 3″, called tiger jaws because of the fang-like hairs along the edges of the gray-green lvs. Large, yellow, daisy-like fls. Culture: 5, 6, or 7; 10; 13; 15–16; 23 with the addition of three parts garden loam. Propagation: 33, preferably spring or fall, 34 in the spring. Uses: 39a or 42.

*FELICIA (fuh LEE shuh). Compositae. Felicia 'Sutton's Azure Blue,' may be treated as an annual or a perennial, 4″; small plants profusely covered with small, azure-blue daisy fls., each with a contrasting yellow disk. Culture: 5 or 6; 9–10; 13; 15–16; 24 or 26. Propagation: Bloom from June onward from a January sowing of seeds in a moderately warm place. Uses: 39 or 42.

FERNS, miniature, see under Adiantum, Pellaea, Pteris and Polystichum.

*FICUS (FYE kus). Moraceae. *F. radicans variegata,* tender evergreen trailer that may be trained up on a small trellis or a moss totem pole, or allowed to ramble along the soil, or over the edges of a hanging basket; beautifully variegated lvs., light green, gray-green, and creamy white, about 1½ inches long by 1 inch wide, *repens pumila*, true miniature creeping fig with puckered, heart-shaped lvs. of deep green, about a half inch long. Excellent as a trailer, or may be trained to climb a moss wall as might be erected in a miniature garden; slow-growing and well-adapted to artistic training, for example as a miniature espalier. (Illustration 75.) Culture: 1, 2, 3, 4, 5, 6, 7, or 8; 10–11; 13–14; 16, 17 or 18; 22 or 26. Propagation: 34. Uses: 39, 40, or 42. *Ficus diversifolia* is an upright miniature fig tree; see Illustration 76. It is perfect as a tree plant for a miniature garden or landscape.

*FITTONIA (fit TOH nee uh). Acanthaceae. *F. verschaffeltii*, TH, 8″, velvety green lvs. with glowing network of bright, rose-pink veins (Illustration 77); var. *argyroneura*, TH, 8″, has slightly smaller lvs. of the same green, perhaps a shade lighter, with white veins. Since these plants spread in a greenhouse, sometimes occupying considerable space, it may be hard to conceive of them as miniature plants. However, they are lovely additions to most window garden terrariums, or as plants for 3-inch pots. Culture: 1, 2, 3, 4, 7, or 8; 10–11; 13–14; 16, 17 or 18; 22 or 29. Propagation: 34. Uses: 38, 39, 40, or 42.

FORSYTHIA (for SITH or SYTH ee uh). Oleaceae. *F. viridissima* var. *bronxensis*, HS, 10–12″, a slow-growing dwarf shrub

ILLUSTRATION 75. Ficus repens pumila, *a miniature creeping fig. (Scale: leaf ½ inch long.)*

with yellow fls. in the spring. A splendid plant to winter in a cold frame, then in January bring to a cool, sunny, moist window or greenhouse for earliest spring bloom. After bloom, prune it back as much as you please; it blooms on the new wood formed after flowering. Culture: 5, 6, 7, or 8; 9 or 10; 13–14; 16 or 17; 26. Propagation: 34. Uses: 39, 41, or 42.

FRAGARIA (fruh GAY ree uh). Rosaceae. *F. indica*, HP, 3″, a trailing plant with bright yellow fls. April to Sept., followed by red fruits. Sometimes known as the Indian strawberry. Culture: 5 or 6; 9–10; 13; 16; 26 with addition of a teaspoon of bone meal to a pot of mix, and one part well-rotted cow manure by volume to the soil mixture. Propagation: 31 or 36 in the spring. Uses: 39, 41, or 42.

FRANKENIA (frank EEN ee uh). Frankeniaceae. *F. laevis*, HP, 1″, mat-forming with fls. of pale pink in July. Culture: 6; 9 in winter; 13; 16–17; 22 or 26. Propagation: 36 in the spring or fall. Uses: 39, 41, or 42.

FUCHSIA (FEW shuh). Onagraceae. *F. magellanica gracilis* var. *variegata*, TH, to 10″ tall, with slender, trailing to semi-upright stems and bright green leaves variegated with white and silver-green; fls. scarlet. *magellanica riccartonii*, TH, 3–8″, is said to be perhaps the hardiest fuchsia; it has purple and scarlet fls. from June to Oct.; var. 'H.T.G. Mutation' is the same but has variegated lvs. *procumbens*, TH, 3″, is a trailer with green lvs., blue and yellow fls. July-Aug., followed

ILLUSTRATION 76. Ficus diversifolia. *(Scale: leaf ¾ inch wide.)*

ILLUSTRATION 77. Fittonia verschaffelti.

by persistent red berries. *pumila*, TH, 9″, forms a compact dwarf plant with bright ruby-red fls. through most of the summer. 'Tom Thumb' is a free-flowering dwarf variety, advertised as being hardy, and bearing beautiful fls. of rose and scarlet. All of these fuchsias require careful pruning (usually in the spring before they are started into active growth) and training to keep them to desirable size and shape for a small indoor garden. Culture: 3, 4, 5, 6, 7, or 8; 9–10; 12 in winter, 13 in spring, 14 in summer, 13 in the fall; 16–17; 22 with addition of one part well-rotted cow manure. Propagation: 31–32, 34 in the spring. Uses: 38, 39, 41, or 42.

*GASTERIA (gas TEER ee uh). Liliaceae. G. *liliputana*, TS, a miniature succulent with oblong lvs. of dark green, spotted with lighter color. Culture: 3, 4, 5, 6, or 7; 10; 12; 15, 16 or 17—fresh air is important; 21 or 24. Propagation: 34. Uses: 39a or 42.

*GAZANIA (guh ZAY nee uh). Compositae. G. 'Bridget,' 6″, a hybrid with large daisy fls. of orange with a black center; 'Freddie,' 6″, hybrid with yellow fls. with green center; 'Roger,' 6″, hybrid with green-centered purple fls.; 'Splendens,' 4″, black-centered orange fls., and 'Sutton's Hybrids,' a magnificent strain of many colors and combinations with extra large fls. on plants about 6″ tall. All of these are tender perennials. Culture: 5 or 6; 9 or 10 in the winter, 11 in the summer and early fall; 12–13; 15, 16, or 17—fresh air is important; 24 or 26. Propagation: 32, 36 in the spring. Uses: 39 or 42. The plants are not winter hardy outdoors except in the deep South and in southern California.

GENTIANA (jen tee AY nuh). Gentianaceae. *G. acaulis,* HP, 4″, beautiful trumpet-shaped fls. of intense dark blue March to May; var. *angustifolia,* HP, 4″, has trumpets of brilliant sapphire blue. *angulosa,* HP, 2″, has deep blue fls. during April and May; needs soil 22 instead of 26. *clusii,* HP 4″, has fls. of deep blue, the throats spotted with olive-green, in June. *farreri,* HP, 4″, has tubular fls. 2 inches long of iridescent blue, white-throated, and appearing Aug. to Oct.; considered an exceptional species. *lagodechiana,* HP, 3″, has rich blue fls., lighter on the outside of the tube, and spotted green in the throat, July-Aug. *macaulayi* Well's variety, HP, 4″, a hybrid with large turquoise-blue fls. Aug. to Nov. *saxosa,* HP, 4″, bronze-green lvs. and large, ivory-white fls. in July, continuing to Sept. *sino-ornata,* HP, 4″, large turquoise-blue fls. in the early fall; soil 22 instead of 26. There are dozens of other miniature gentians, some of them even smaller than those described here. However, all of these are available; after you obtain a measure of success with the species listed here, begin to search out some of the others. Culture: 6; 9; 12 in winter, other times 13–14; 16–17; 26 with addition of one part grit or chipped limestone, except for species indicated otherwise. Propagation: 31, 36 in early spring. Uses: 41 or 42.

GERANIUM (jer RAY nee um). Geraniaceae. *G dalmaticum,* HP, 3″, a neat, small plant with large, satiny fls. of pink in the spring or summer. *Renardii,* HP, 6″, deep-veined lvs. and a profusion of red-veined, pale pink fls. *sessiflora nigra,* HP, 4″, a small, brown-leaved plant with white fls. *subcaulescens,* HP, 6″, long-flowering plant with fls. of carmine, each centered by a shiny, black eye. *sanguineum* var. 'Alpenglow,' HP, 6″, a prostrate plant with a long season of dark, red fls. Culture: 5 or 6; 9; 12 in winter, 13 other times; 16–17; 26 with addition of one part compost or well-rotted cow manure. Propagation: 31–32, 36 spring or fall. Uses: 39, 41, or 42.

GERANIUMS, miniature, varieties of house geranium (*Pelargonium hortorum*), see Chapter 7.

*GESNERIA (gez NEER ee uh). Gesneriaceae. *G. cuneifolia*, TH, to 6″ in diameter by 3 or 4 inches tall. Lvs. of bright, grass-green from 1 to 2 inches long, and a constant display of 1-inch long scarlet-red fls., each a slender tube. Culture: 3, 4, 5, 6, 7, or 8; 10–11; 13–14; 16, 17 or 18; 22, 27, 28, or 29. Propagation: 33 or 36. Uses: 40 or 42.

GEUM (JEE um). Rosaceae. *G. montanum*, HP, 6″, golden-yellow fls. in early summer, followed by silken seedheads. *rhaeticum*, 6″, has pink fls. May-June. Culture: 6; 9 in winter; 13; 16–17; 22, 24, or 26. Propagation: 30 or 31, or 36 in the spring or fall. Uses: 39, 41, or 42.

GLECOMA (glee KOH muh). Labiatae. *G. hederacea variegata*, syn. *Nepeta hederacea variegata*, HP, ground ivy; a trailing plant, sometimes weedy in the outdoor garden, that makes a choice, small plant for a basket in a sunny window; blue fls. in the summer. Culture: 3, 4, 5, 6, 7, or 8; 9–10; 13–14; 15–16; 24, or 26. Propagation: 33 or 34. Uses: 38. (See Illustration 63.)

GLOBULARIA (glob yew LAY ree uh). Globulariaceae. *G. bellidifolia*, HP, 2″, tuft-forming evergreen rosettes with blue fls. in the summer. *cordifolia*, HP, 3″, evergreen rosettes with heads of silver-blue fls. June-Aug. *incanescens*, HP, 3″, evergreen rosettes of blue-green lvs. with blue fls. in June. Cul-

ILLUSTRATION 78. Gesneria *'Lemon Drop,'* an everblooming hybrid of Gesneria cuneifolia. *(Scale: each flower ¾ inch long.)*

ture: 6; 9 in the winter; 12; 16–17 in the summer, but better 19 at other times; 26 with addition of one part chipped limestone. Propagation: 30 or 31, or 36 in the spring or fall. Uses: 39, 41, or 42.

GLOXINIA, miniature, see Chapter 2.

GOMPHRENA (gom FREE nuh). Amaranthaceae. *G. globosa nana compacta* 'Buddy,' HHA, 6″, uniform ball-shaped plants covered with fls. of vivid purple. Culture: 5 or 6; 10–11; 13; 15–16; 24 or 26. Propagation: 32. Uses: 42.

*GYMNOCALYCIUM (gym noh kal ISS ee um). Cactaceae. *G. bruchii*, TC, 1″, a tiny miniature cactus that flowers when less than 1 inch across; the fls. of pale pink are the size of a quarter. The plants form clusters 2 to 3 inches in diameter. Most other gymnocalyciums are desirable for culture 39a or 42. Culture: 5, 6, or 7; 10–11; 12; 15; 21. Propagation: 31, 34 in summer. Uses: 39a or 42.

GYPSOPHILA (gyp SOFF ill uh). Caryophyllaceae. *G. cerastioides*, HP, 2–3″, dark green lvs. form tufts from which red-veined white fls. rise from May to Sept. *fratensis*, syn. *repens*, HP, 6″, a trailing plant with fls. of pale pink during the summer. *muralis*, HHA, 6″, downy lvs. and stems, much-branched and covered with bell flowers of rose-pink in the summer and fall. Culture: 5 or 6; 9–10; 12–13; 16; 24 with addition of old mortar or chipped brick; 31, 32, 34, or 36 in the spring. Uses: 38, 39, 41, or 42.

ILLUSTRATION 79. Gesneria saxatilis *has tiny, glossy dark green holly-shaped leaves and branches into a miniature shrub with red flowers. (Scale: flower ¾ inch long.)*

HABERLEA (hay ber LEE ah). Gesneriaceae. *H. ferdinandi-coburgii*, HP, 4–6″, stiff rosette of dark green lvs. and white and lilac fls. in May. *rhodopensis*, HP, 6″, is similar, with fls. from May to June. Both are closely allied to the ramonda. Culture: 4; 9; 12 in winter, 13 other times; 16–17, except 19 in winter; 22. Propagation: 31 or 36 in the spring. Uses: 41a or 42.

*HATIORA (hat ee OH ruh). Cactaceae. *H. salicornioides*, TC, is a small, much-branched plant with the texture and coloring of mistletoe. Each branchlet is bottle-shaped, and thus the plant gets its popular name of drunkard's dream. In the winter and spring it has flowers at the tips of the leaves—iridescent apricot-yellow, each about ¾″ across, and remaining nearly closed on cloudy days. Culture: 3, 4, 5, 6, or 7; 10–11; 13; 15; 16, or 17; 24. Propagation: 34. Uses, 38, 39a, or 42.

*HAWORTHIA (ha WORTH ee uh). Liliaceae. *H. cymbiformis*, TS, 2″. *limifolia*, TS, a small succulent sometimes called fairy washboard because of the transverse ribbing across its leaves (Illustration 80). *marginata*, TS, 4″. *margaritifera*, TS, 3″.

ILLUSTRATION 80. Haworthia limifolia.

ILLUSTRATION 81. Haworthia pilifera, *a miniature succulent.*

minima, TS, a dwarf plant with fat, pointed, green windowed leaves; it forms rosettes of these. *radula,* TS, small, rosette-forming plant (Illustration 81). *reinwordtii,* TS, 2″ *setata,* TS, 2″, a close rosette of slender, pointed lvs. Also, many other small-growing haworthia species and varieties—the list could be nearly endless. Culture: 3 or 4; 9; 13–14; 15–16; 24. Propagation: 33 or 36. Uses: 39a or 42.

HEDERA, miniature and small forms of English ivy, see Chapter 8.

HEERIA, see under Heterocentron.

HELIANTHEMUM (heal ee ANTH ee mum). Cistaceae. *H. alpestre,* HP, 3″, evergreen, gray-green lvs. and yellow fls. *lunulatum,* HP, 2″, a cushion alpine with yellow fls., each petal having an orange spot at the base. Culture: 6; 9 in the winter; 13; 16–17; 21 or 24. Propagation: 31, or 36 in the spring or fall. Uses: 39, 41, or 42.

HELICHRYSUM (hell ee KRISS um). Compositae. *H. bellidioides,* HP, 3″, a ground-hugging plant of silver lvs. with white, everlasting fls. in the summer. *marginatum,* HP, 3″, is a tiny plant that forms hummocks of silver-leaved rosettes and produces white fls., the buds a bright rose-pink. Culture: same as helianthemum, except in a richer soil mixture, such as 26.

*HELXINE (hell ZYE nee). Urticaceae. *H. solierolii,* an almost-hardy trailing plant (1–2″) with tiny, almost translucent succulent stems, and round leaves of bright green. Baby's tears. (Illustration 82). Culture: 1, 2, 3, 4, 5, 6, 7, or 8; 9, 10, or 11; 13–14; 16, 17 or 18; 26, 27 or 29. Propagation: 36. Uses: 38, 39, 40, or 42.

HETEROCENTRON (het er oh CEN tron). Melastomataceae. *H. roseum,* syn. *Heerie rosea,* TH, 2–3″, a carpeting or trailing plant with bright green lvs. and fls. of brilliant magenta-purple through the spring and summer. Culture: 3, 4, 5, 6, 7, or 8; 10–11; 13; 16–17; 22 or 29. Propagation: 36 in the spring. Uses: 38, 39, or 42.

*HIBISCUS (hi BISS kus). Malvaceae. *H. rosa-sinensis,* the Chinese hibiscus, blooms on current wood and does not resent hard pruning. It is possible, therefore, to start with young,

ILLUSTRATION 82. Helxine soleirolii *or baby's-tears. Compare with look-alikes in Illustrations 84 and 89. (Scale: 2-inch pot.)*

rooted cuttings of any of the hybrid varieties, and to prune and train them to be compact mounds or shrublets under 10 inches. Culture: 3, 4, 5, 6, or 7; 10–11; 13; 16 or 17—fresh air is important; 22, 24, or 26. Propagation: 34. Uses: 42.

HOMALOMENA (hoh mal oh MEE nuh). Araceae. *H. humilis*, TH, a rosette of dark green, lanceolate lvs. *sulcata*, TH, has rosettes of heart-shaped lvs., green with a metallic sheen. *wallisii*, TH, has handsome lvs. of green, splashed or marbled with creamy yellow. Culture: 3, 4, 7, or 8; 11; 13–14; 15, 16, 17 or 18; 22, 25, 27, or 29. Propagation: 34. Uses: 40.

HOUSTONIA (hews TOH nee uh). Rubiaceae. *H. caerulea*, HP, 4–6″, known popularly as bluets; a delicate but tough little plant with blue fls. May through July. Culture: 3, 4, 5, or 6; 9 in winter; 13; 15, 16, or 17; 24. Propagation: 30, or 36 in the autumn. Uses: 39, 41, or 42.

*HOYA (HOY ah). Asclepiadaceae. *H. bella*, TH, the miniature wax plant. It forms a bushy, hanging plant with white-centered, blush-pink, fragrant fls. over a long period of time. Culture: 3, 4, 5, 6, or 7; 10–11; 13; 15–16; 22. Propagation: 34, using cuttings of previous year's growth in the spring. Uses: 38. Prune to shape in February, but leave the old flower stalks, for it is from these that more blooms will come.

HYDRANGEA (hy DRAN jee uh). Saxifragaceae. Michael Haworth-Booth in his book *The Hydrangeas* (published in this country by Charles T. Branford Company, Newton Centre, Massachusetts), describes the complete procedure for growing miniature hydrangeas. Briefly, here is the challenging process: Small adventitious flower buds are used as cuttings. These buds are usually produced by plants grown from cuttings of wood that flowered the previous season. When these root, the flowers expand in miniature size, blooming with a ruff of two leaves at their base, and at a total height of 2 inches. Once bloom is gone, no further growth can be made. A satisfying accomplishment for any gardener!

HYPERICUM (high PEER ikum). Hypericaceae. *H. empetrifolium prostratum*, HP, 2″, mat-forming with wee panicles of orange-yellow fls. June to Aug. *fragile*, HP, 4″, has glaucous lvs. and summer fls. of yellow. *repens*, HP, 3″, has yellow fls. in the summer. *reptans*, HP, 3″, has trailing growth and deep yellow fls. June-Sept. *trichocaulon*, HP, 3″, is mat-forming with dense growth of small, bright green lvs. and fls. of vivid red in the bud, but opening to light yellow July-Aug. Culture: 6; 9 in winter; 13; 16–17; 22 or 26. Propagation: 30 or 31, or 34. Uses: 41 or 42.

*HYPOESTES (high poh ESS teez). Acanthaceae. *H. sanguinolenta* var. 'Splash,' TH with dark green lvs. heavily spotted and splashed with bright pink. Pinch back freely to keep as compact mound under 5″. Culture: 3, 4, 5, 7, or 8; 10–11; 13–14; 16; 22, 27, or 29. Propagation: 34. Uses: 39 or 42.

HYPOXIS (high POX iss). Amaryllidaceae. *H. stellata elegans*, TH, 6–12″, white fls. in the spring, marked in the center with a conspicuous star of contrasting color. A greenhouse perennial that grows from a corm. Culture: 5 or 6; 9; 13 when in growth, 12 other times; 16–17; 22. Propagation: 36 at repotting time. Uses: 42.

IBERIS (eye BEER iss). Cruciferae. *I. saxatilis*, HP, 4–6″, forms little bushes that are smothered with white, tinged purple, fls. Indoors these appear in late winter and spring. Culture: 5 or 6; 9; 12–13; 16; 21. Propagation: 31, 34, 36 spring or fall. Uses: 39, 41, or 42.

*IMPATIENS (im PAY shenz). Balsaminaceae. *I. sultanii* var. 'Red Herold,' HHP, a very dwarf variety, almost creeping, occasionally reaching as high as 5". Dark, nearly black-green foliage is nearly covered by the large, fiery scarlet fls. Culture: 2, 3, 4, 5, 6, 7, or 8; 10–11; 13–14; 16–17; 22, 24, 26, 27, or 29. Propagation: 33, 34. Uses: 38 or 42.

IRIS (EYE riss). Iridaceae. *I. cristata*, HP, 3–6", has miniature iris fans of lvs. and May. fls. of powder-blue, with a touch of orange. *flavissima*, HP, 3", narrow small lvs. and yellow fls. in the spring. *lacustris*, HP, 3", miniature leaf fans, and pale blue fls. in May. Culture: 5 or 6; 9 in the winter; 12 in late summer, and not harmful during winter, but 13–14 during spring and early summer; 16–17; 24; or 26. Propagation: 35. Uses: 39, 41, or 42.

JANKAE (JANK ee uh). Gesneriaceae. *J. heldreichii*, HP, 2–3", with rosettes of hairy lvs. and stems of four- or five-petaled lavender-lilac fls. in early summer; var. *alba* is the same, but has white fls. Culture as for ramonda, which see.

JASMINUM (JAZZ min um). Oleaceae. *J. parkeri*, HP, 10–12", a hardy shrublet with yellow fls. June-July. Culture: 5 or 6; 9–10; 13; 16–17; 22. Propagation: 34, inserted in cold frame in autumn. Uses: 42. Prune to shape after flowering, but try to leave those shoots that have not flowered.

*KALANCHOE (kal an KOH ee). Crassulaceae. *K.* 'Tom Thumb,' TS, 8", with scarlet-red fls. in the winter. 'Yellow Tom Thumb,' is the same but has apricot-yellow fls. 'Scarlet Gnome,' 7", is more compact than the others, forming a lower mound, and providing larger flowers. Culture: 4, 5, 6, or 7; 10–11; 13; 15–16; 24 or 26 with addition of one part well-rotted cow manure. Propagation: 32. Uses: 37, if budded growth tips 1 to 2 inches long are rooted in early winter; also 39a and 42.

KOELLIKERIA (kerr lick EER ee uh). Gesneriaceae. *K. erinoides*, TH, 10", available recently for the first time in this country. A highly desirable gesneriad, requiring culture as for achimenes, except it forms a basal rosette of leaves, and therefore does not require pinching. Airy sprays of white and purple flowers in the summer seldom exceed 10".

*KOHLERIA (koh LEER ee uh). Gesneriaceae. *K. amabilis*, TH, has silver-green hairy lvs. marked with chocolate-brown veins; it has tubular fls. of pink, brightly dotted with red. *lindeniana* has bronze and green leaves, dashingly veined with silver-white. The fragrant fls. are white with a throat of lavender-blue that sometimes extends to within a half inch of the petal edges. Both of these plants reach maturity at about 12″ under normal conditions, though I have seen plants of *amabilis* blooming in splendor at 36″. To grow smaller plants, put one scaly rhizome in a 3-inch pot; if it receives proper light and other growing conditions, it should flower at or below 10″. It is possible, also, to make tip cuttings of budded growth which may be rooted in warmth and high humidity. They will usually come into flower without any difficulty, thus forming a short, compact plant crowned with fls. Culture: 3, 4, 5, 6, 7, or 8; 10–11; 13; 15, 16 or 17; 22, 27, 28, or 29. Propagation: 33, 34, or 36 after flowering season ends. Uses: 39, 40, or 42.

*LACHENALIA (lack en AY lee uh). Liliaceae. *L. glaucina*, HHP, 6″, fragrant fls. of steel-blue. *pallida*, HHP, 6″, white fls. Both species are bulbous. Culture: 3, 4, 5, 6, 7, or 8; 10; 13; 15–16; 24. Propagation: 33. Uses: 39 or 42.

LAVANDULA (luh VAN dew luh). Labiatae. Lavender. *L. atropurpurea nana*, low-growing variety of lavender. *nana compacta pacta* even smaller, and an excellent choice for a cool, sunny window garden of herbs. Culture: 5 or 6; 9–10; 13; 16; 24. Propagation: 34 in sandy soil in early fall. Uses: 42. Prune or clip as necessary to keep compact.

LINARIA (lin AY ree uh). Scrophulariaceae. *L. aequitriloba*, HP, 1″, a tiny creeping evergreen plant with minute violet fls. July to September. *alpina*, HP, 5″, has compact-growing gray lvs. and violet and orange fls. through most of the summer. Culture: 5 or 6; 9–10; 13; 16–17; 24. Propagation: 31. Uses: 41 or 42.

LINUM (LYE num). Linaceae. Flax, *L. elegans*, HP, ground-hugging plant with yellow fls., recommended for pot culture. *flavum compactum*, HP, 6″, is a free-blooming plant with fls. of bright yellow in the summer. Culture: 5 or 6; 9–10; 13; 16; 22. Propagation: 31 or 36 in the spring. Uses: 41 or 42.

*LITHOPS (LITH ops). Aizoaceae. Countless species of this tender plant are desirable for a miniature garden of cacti and succulents. For example, *L. salicola* has bodies of pale olive-green and white, daisy-like fls. ¾″ in diameter. Culture: 5 or 6; 10–11; 12; 15–16; 21. Propagation: 33 or 36. Uses: 39a or 42.

LOBELIA (low BEE lee uh). Lobeliaceae. *L. erinus pumila* 'Snowball,' HHA, 4″, a mound-forming dwarf plant, covered through the summer with butterfly-like fls. of pure white; var. 'Rosamond,' HHA, 4–6″, has fls. of deep, carmine-red with a contrasting eye of white. Both of these may be flowered in late winter and early spring when grown indoors. Culture: 5 or 6; 9–10; 13–14; 16; 26. Culture: 33. Uses: 38, 39, or 42.

*LOBIVIA (loh BIH vee uh). Cactaceae. *L. larabei*, TC, a cluster-forming plant with luminous red fls. larger than itself. Blooms even when it is small. *paucartambensis*, TC, plants up to 1½ inches in diameter, freely producing offsets which root into the surrounding soil while still attached to the mother plant; it has fls. of bright crimson from spring to fall. Also desirable, these species of *Lobivia: aurea, binghamiana, leucomalla, cylindrica, rossii, corbula* and *backebergii*. Culture: 5, 6, or 7; 10–11; 13; 15–16; 21. Propagation: 33 or 36. Uses: 39a or 42.

*LOBULARIA (lob yew LAY ree uh). Cruciferae. Sweet alyssum. *L. maritima minimum californica*, HA, 3″, mounds of pure white fls.; var. 'Little Dorritt,' HA, 3″, forms little bushes of miniature white fls. These are small forms of the sweet alyssum commonly cultivated in outdoor gardens. They are useful indoors, particularly in a cool, sunny greenhouse or for bedding outside. Culture: 3, 4, 5, 6, 7, or 8; 9–10 or 11; 13; 15, 16 or 17; 22, 24, or 26. Propagation: 33. Uses: 37, 38, 39, 41, or 42.

LYCHNIS (LICK niss). Caryophyllaceae. *L. alpina*, HP, 6″, fls. of rose-pink in the summer. *lagascae*, HP, 3″, silver-green lvs. and fls. of carmine-rose through most of the summer. Culture: 5, 6, or 7; 10; 12; 16; 26. Propagation: 31 or 36 spring or fall. Uses: 39, 41a, or 42.

MALPIGHIA (mal PIG ee uh). Malpighiaceae. *M. coccigera*, tender shrublet with oval, holly-like small lvs. of bright, glossy green. It has light pink, delicate fls. (Illustration 83.) Cul-

ILLUSTRATION 83. Malpighia coccigera. *(Scale: 3-inch pot.)*

ture: 5, 6, 7, or 8; 10–11; 13 in winter, 14 summer; 16–17; 22. Propagation: 34 in summer. Uses: 39 or 42. Prune as necessary to keep to desired size and shape.

MANETTIA (muh NEE she uh). Rubiaceae. *M. bicolor*, TH, trailing stems set with small bright green lvs. and yielding spring fls. of waxy, bright yellow and red. They are tubular, sometimes giving the plant a common name of firecracker bush. Culture: 3, 4, 5, 6, or 8; 10; 13; 16–17, but fresh air is important; 22. Propagation: 34. Uses: 38 or 42.

*MAMMILLARIA (mam mil LAY ree uh). Cactaceae. *M baumii*, TC, heads 1″ in diameter, forming pincushions with tender, harmless spines of pale yellow, and yellow fls. during the summer. *elongata*, TC, 3″, is larger, and has yellow fls. in the summer. *multiceps*, TC, is a tiny species with cream-white fls. followed by scarlet berries, and it bears endless numbers of offsets. Also, for miniature gardens: countless other mammillarias. Culture: 5, 6, or 7; 10; 13 spring and summer, 12 other times, even completely dry Jan. and Feb.; 15–16; 20 with one equal part rough, chipped mortar and powdered brick added. Propagation: 32 or 34 in the spring. Uses: 39a or 42.

MARANTA (muh RANT uh). Marantaceae. *M. oppenheimiana tricolor*, TH, a small variety with rainbow-hued leaves of great brilliancy. Culture: 1, 2, 3, 4, or 8; 10–11; 14 spring and summer, 13 in fall, 12 dead of winter except under fluorescent lights, then 13 in winter; 16, 17 or 18; 22, 27, or 29. Propagation: 36 in early spring. Uses: 40 or 42.

MARIGOLDS, miniature and dwarf, see Tagetes.

MAZUS (MAY zus). Scrophulariaceae. *M. pumila*, HP, ½", a dwarf, trailing plant with bright green lvs. and lilac and violet fls. May through summer. *reptans*, HP, 1", has fls. that embrace the colors rose-lavender, brown and white, May-Oct. Culture: 5 or 6; 9–10; 13; 16–17; 21 or 24. Propagation: 31 or 36 in the spring. Uses: 39, 41, or 42.

MENTHA (MEN tha). Labiatae. *M. requienii*, HP, ½", a minute carpeting plant with green lvs. that have a strong peppermint aroma. It has tiny mauve fls. in the summer. Corsican mint. Illustration 84. Culture: 2, 3, 4, or 8; 9–10; 13–14; 15, 16 or 17; 24 or 26. Propagation: 34. Uses: 38, 39, or 41.

MIMULUS (MIM yew luss). Scrophulariaceae. *M. primuloides*, HP, 3", has carpets of yellow fls. in May. 'Red Emperor,' HHA, 4–6", forms a compact mound covered with large fls. of crimson-scarlet; when wintered in a greenhouse, may be treated as a tender perennial. Culture: 6; 9–10; 13; 16–17; 24 with addition of one part well-rotted cow manure. Propagation: 31 at 55 to 65°. Uses: 42.

*MONANTHES (moh NANTH eez). Crassulaceae. *M. muralis*, TS, 2–3", a dwarf succulent that forms tiny bushes. They often take on artistic shapes that remind one of ancient bonsai creations. This species bears a quantity of yellow fls. with a wide disk on thread-like pedicels (Illustrations 85

ILLUSTRATION 84. Mentha requienii, *the Corsican mint. Compare with Illustrations 82 and 89; all three plants are similar in appearance and often confused. (Scale: each leaf ¼ inch across.)*

ILLUSTRATION 85. Mo-
nanthes muralis, *a
miniature succulent.*

ILLUSTRATION 86. Monanthes polyphylla. *(Scale: 2-inch pot.)*

and 86). *polyphylla*, TS, ½" tall, looks like a miniature form
of old-fashioned hen and chicken (sempervivum). In the
winter and spring these wee rosettes send up odd, yellow
fls. on threadlike pedicels. Both of these species need a
sandy soil on the dry side; they will rot and die in moist
humus and high humidity. Culture: 5, 6, or 7; 10–11; 12; 15–
16; 20 or 24. Propagation: 34. Uses: 37, 39a, or 42.

MUEHLENBECKIA (mew len BECK ee uh). Polyganaceae. *M. nana*,
HP, 6", a mat-forming carpeter with small, dark green lvs.
axillaris, 3", a creeping, mat-forming species, is sometimes
cultivated. Culture: 5, 6, or 7; 9–10; 13; 15–16; 24 or 26.
Propagation: 34. Uses: 38.

MYOSOTIS (my oh so tiss). Boraginaceae. *M. hybrida* Star of
Love, HP, 6", a low-growing, large-flowered variety of vibrant
blue color. Culture: 5 or 6; 9–10; 13; 16–17; 22, 24, or 26.
Propagation: 31 or 32, the seedlings treated as biennials
and brought into bloom in ten to twelve months from sowing. Uses: 42.

*NEMATANTHUS (nee muh TANTH us). Gesneriaceae. *N. wett-
steinii* has shiny, dark green leaves and pouched or gold-
fish-like orange and yellow flowers. Illustration 87. Treat as
Codonanthe.

NEMESIA (nuh MEE she uh). Scrophulariaceae. *N.* 'Carter's
Dwarf Large-flowered Rainbow,' a hybrid strain of all colors
and shades, maturing at 6 to 8". Available as a mixture or by

ILLUSTRATION 87. Nematanthus wettsteinii. *(Scale: flower ¾ inch long.)*

named varieties: 'Blue Gem,' 'Fire King,' 'White Gem' and 'Orange Prince.' Culture: 6; 9; 13; 16–17; 22, 24, or 26. Propagation: 31 in Jan. or Feb. at 65–72°. Uses: 42 for a cool, sunny greenhouse.

NEOMARICA (nee oh MAIR ick uh). Iridaceae. *N. northiana* var. *variegata* is a most unusual variegated form that tends to be miniature. Its appearance is very appealing among other plants. Illustration 88. Treat as *Acorus,* but not quite so much water.

NEPETA, species *hederaceae variegata,* a synonym for Glecoma (which see), used as much, if not more in the trade.

ILLUSTRATION 88. Neomarica northiana *var.* variegata, *the variegated walking iris. (Scale: 2-inch pot.)*

ILLUSTRATION 89. Nertera depressa. *Compare with Illustrations 82 and 84. (Scale: 2-inch pot.)*

NERTERA (NER ter uh). Rubiaceae. *N. granadensis,* syn. *N. depressa,* HHP, 1", the bead plant or fruiting duckweed. Small, carpeting leaves, and fls. followed by showy orange-red berries that persist for several months. (Illustration 89.) Culture: 1, 2, 3, 4, or 8; 10 spring and summer, 9 fall and winter; 13 Oct. to March, 14 other times; 16, 17 or 18; 26. Propagation: 32 at 55–65°, or 36 in the spring. Uses: 40, 41a, or 42.

NIEREMBERGIA (near em BERJ ee uh). Solanaceae. *N. hippomanica* var. *caerulea,* HHA, 3–12", a mound-forming plant covered with delicate lavender-blue fls. with contrasting center eyes of clear yellow. *patagonica,* HP, 1", a carpeter with pink fls. in the summer. *repens,* syn. *rivularis,* HP, 1", a carpeter with white fls. in the summer. Culture for HHA species and varieties: 2, 3, 4, or 8; 10; 13 in winter, 14 at other times; 16–17; 26 with addition of one part well-rotted cow manure. Propagation: 33, preferably in winter or early spring at 60–65°, or 34 in late summer. Uses: 38 or 42. Culture for HP species: 6, 9–10; 13; 16–17; 24. Propagation: 33 in winter or early spring at 55–65°, or 34 in late summer. Uses: 39, 41, 41a, or 42.

*NOTOCACTUS (noh toh KAK tuss). Cactaceae. *N. leninghausii,* TC, 3" tall at 5 years of age with golden spines and fls. of powdery yellow. Most species of notocactus are valuable for 39a or 42; some of these are *apricus, concinnus, hasel-*

bergii, mammulosus, ottonis, spiralis rutilans and *scopa.*
Culture as for gymnocalycium.

OENOTHERA (ee no THEER uh). Onagraceae. *O. caespitosa,* HP,
4–9″, with fragrant, white fls. in July. 'Millard's Variety,'
HP, 6″, with large, golden-yellow fls. *nuttallii,* HP, 6–9″, pink
or white fls. in the summer. *ovata,* HP, 6″, rich yellow fls. in
May. *pumila,* HP, 6″ continuous summer fls. of bright,
golden-yellow. Culture: 5 or 6; 9 in winter; 13–14; 16–17; 26
with addition of one part well-rotted cow manure. Propagation: 31 or 32, 34 in spring or summer, or 36 in early spring.
Uses: 39, 41, or 42.

OMPHALODES (om fal OH deez). Boraginaceae. *O. verna,* HP, 6″,
the creeping forget-me-not; one of the plants called blue-
eyed mary. Fls. in the spring. Culture: 4, 9; 13–14; 16; 22.
Propagation: 31 or 36 in early spring. Uses: 39, 41, or 42.

*OPUNTIA (oh POONT she uh). Cactaceae. O. 'Maverick,' TC,
fleshy, small lvs. of bright, almost golden green, densely
dotted with sulfur-yellow glochids. *microdasys albata,* TC, is
similar to 'Maverick,' but covered with snow-white glochids.
Culture: 5, 6, or 7; 9, 10 or 11; 13 spring and summer, 12 in
fall and winter; 15–16; 20 or 21 with addition of one equal
part chipped mortar and brick fragments. Propagation: 32,
or 34 in summer. Uses: 39a or 42.

OREOCHARIS (oh ree OCK are iss). Gesneriaceae. *O. primuloides,*
HP, 6″, a beautiful plant closely related to the ramonda, and

ILLUSTRATION 90. Oxalis
hedysaroides rubra,
*the firefern. (Scale: 3-
inch pot.)*

sending forth mauve fls. June and July. Culture: see ramonda.

*OSMANTHUS (OZ MANTH us). Oleaceae. *O. ilicifolius variegatus*,
HP, a small, bushy shrub with holly-like leaves of gray-green,
broadly margined and splashed with cream-white. Culture:
5 or 6; 9–10; 13; 15, 16 or 17, but fresh air is important;
22. Uses: 39 or 42. Prune as necessary at intervals of 3 or 4
months to keep the plant shapely and compact.

*OXALIS (ox uh liss). Oxalidaceae. *O. adenophylla*, 3″, cut lvs.
and large lilac-pink fls. May and June. *Bowieana*, 3–6″, rose-
purple fls. in the fall. *braziliensis*, 6″, large fls. of intense
purple from May to July. *carnosa*, 6″, yellow fls. in the fall.
cernua, 6–12″, yellow, large, single fls. during winter and
spring; var. *flore pleno* or 'Caprina,' has large, fully double
fls. *enneaphylla*, 2″, gray lvs. in rosette formation, and large
fls. of pure white in May and June. *hedysaroides rubra* (see
Illustration 90) 2–10″, the firefern; lvs. of glowing burgundy
with tiny fls. of rich, butter-yellow; may be grown to tree
form; this species is hard to beat for planting in an almost-
closed terrarium where it has constant light, warmth and
moisture; trim and pinch to encourage compactness. *herrerae*, small lvs. that turn deep bronze-red in hot sunlight;
it has tiny fls. of yellow. *hirta*, 3–6″, red fls. in the summer.
inops, 2–3″, a neat small plant with vibrant, rose-pink fls.
lobata, 3″, a choice species with golden-yellow fls. *magel-*

ILLUSTRATION 91. Oxalis martiana aureo-reticulata; *same culture as* O. regnellii. *(Scale: 2-inch pot.)*

lanica, 1″, a carpeting plant with bronzy lvs. and white fls. throughout the summer. *melanosticta,* 3″, compact, mound- or rosette-forming, the lvs. and stems covered with silvery white down, and sending up yellow fls. in the fall. *regnellii,* 6–10″, dark reddish green, square-cut lvs. and large white fls.; grows from a scaly rhizome and blooms winter and spring. *rubra (crassipes* or *rosea),* 6–12″, tuberous-rooted species with bright pink fls. winter or summer. *variabilis,* 3–6″, rose- red, white or pink fls. in the fall. Culture for *enneaphylla:* 5 or 6; 9; 13, except dry after foliage matures in summer and until growth is started in the fall; 16; 25. Propagation: 36 at time of repotting in the fall. Uses: 42. Culture for *hirta:* 5, 6, or 7; 9, 10, or 11; 13 except in fall and winter while dormant, dry and cool; 16; 21, 24, or 26. Propagation: 36 at time of repotting in March or April. Uses: 42. Culture for *herrerae:* 5, 6, or 7; 10–11; 13; 16; 24 or 26. Propagation: 34. Uses: 38 for hanging basket, or 42; not an outstanding species, but easy to grow. Culture for *hedysaroides rubra:* 1, 2, 3, 4, 5, 6, 7, or 8; 10; 13–14; 16, 17 or 18; 22, 26, 27, or 29. Propagation: 34. Uses: 40 or 42. Culture for *adenophylla, braziliensis* and *inops:* 5 or 6; 9, 10 or 11; 13, except dry after foliage matures in summer, and until growth is started in the fall; 16; 21. Propagation: 36 at time of repotting in early fall. Uses: 42; also 38 for *braziliensis.* Culture for *bowieana, carnosa* and *cernua:* 5, 6, or 7; 9, 10 or 11; 13 except dry and cool when dormant spring and early sum- mer; 15, 16, or 17; 21, 24, or 26. Propagation: 36 at time of repotting in the summer: 38 or 42. Culture of *magellanica:* 5, 6, or 7; 9; 13, except in fall and winter while dormant and dry; 16; 25. Propagation: 36 at time of repotting in March or April. Uses: 39a or 42. Culture of *regnellii* and *rubra:* 3, 4, 5, 6, or 7; 10–11; 13 except for resting period in summer, then grown as 12; 15–16; 22, 24, or 26. Propagation: 36, preferably in summer or fall. Uses: 38 or 42. Culture for *lobata, melano- sticta* and *variabilis:* 5 or 6; 9, 10 or 11; 13, except dry and cool after foliage matures in winter or spring, and until started into growth in Aug.; 16; 21 or 25. Propagation: 36 at time of repotting. Uses: 42.

*PACHYVERIA (pack ee VEER ee uh). Crassulaceae. P. 'Starlight,' is a bigeneric hybrid of pachyphytum and echeveria. A pleasing new plant that forms 2" rosettes of thick, spoon-shaped chalk-white lvs. Culture as for echeveria.

*PAROCHETUS (pair oh KEY tus). Leguminosae. *P. communis,* the blue oxalis, a hardy perennial with shamrock-like lvs., marked at the base with a reddish brown crescent, and dime- to nickel-size fls. of cobalt blue, produced from the leaf axils. Culture: 3, 4, 5, 6, or 7; 10–11; 13, 15 or 16; 24 with one-fourth part well-rotted cow manure if possible. Propagation: 36. Uses: 38 or 42.

PARONYCHIA (pair oh NYE kee uh). Caryophyllaceae. *P. nivea,* HP, 3", a carpeting plant that thrives in hot, dry situations, and sends forth silver bracts in the summer. Culture: 6 or 7; 11; 12; 15–16; 24. Propagation: 32 or 36 in spring or fall. Uses: 39a or 42.

PELARGONIUM, miniature and semidwarf varieties, see Chapter 7.

*PELECYPHORA (pell ee sye FOH ruh). Cactaceae. *P. aselliformis,* TC, a rare plant to 1½" in diameter, and 4" tall, that resembles a mammillaria, and bears bright fls. of purple-pink. Culture: 5, 6, or 7; 10; 13 spring and summer, 12 in fall, even drier in winter; 15–16; 20 or 23. Propagation: 32 or 34 in the spring. Uses: 39a or 42.

*PELLIONIA (pell ee OH nee uh). Urticaceae. *P. daveauana,* TH, creeping or trailing plant cultivated for its handsome foliage; the lvs. are broadly margined with chocolate-brown, with the balance of the area silver-green; some lvs. are entirely brown. *pulchra,* TH, silver-green lvs. boldly veined with reddish brown. Culture: 3, 4, 5, 6, 7, or 8; 10–11; 13; 15, 16, 17 or 18; 26 or 29. Propagation: 34. Uses: 38 or 40. Trim as necessary to keep plants in bounds.

PENSTEMON (PEN stem on). Scrophulariaceae. *P. cristatus,* HP, 3", fls. of violet-purple in May. *menziesii,* HP, 5–6", evergreen foliage and purple-blue fls. June, July, sometimes into Aug. *rupicola,* HP, 2–4", glaucous mound-forming with red fls. May-Aug., needs some shade; var. *alba* is the same but has white fls. Culture: 6; 9 in the winter; 13; 16; 26 with

ILLUSTRATION 92. Pellaea rotundifolia *is a small-growing fern for a shaded, moist place with moderate temperatures. (Scale: one frond 5 inches long.)*

ILLUSTRATION 93. *'Pixie' peperomia (at left) compared with standard size variety. (Scale: larger pot is 3 inches across.)*

addition of one part well-rotted cow manure. Propagation: 30, or 36 in early spring. Uses: 39, 41, 42.

*PEPEROMIA (pepper OH mee uh). Piperaceae. *P. caperata* var. 'Little Fantasy,' TH, grows as a rosette of heart-shaped lvs. deeply quilted and dark, almost black-green; grow as a miniature while young, and when it gets too large, start a new plant. *japonica*, TH, has rounded lvs. in dense formation, a highly decorative little plant, often topped by green catkin-like fls. *nivalis*, TH, a small plant of clustering, upright rosettes. 'Pixie,' TH, with small succulent lvs. of bright green,

ILLUSTRATION 94. Peperomia rubella. *(Scale: 3-inch pot.)*

ILLUSTRATION 95. Peperomia angulata. *(Scale: 3-inch pot.)*

forming dense bushlets of stems clustering from the base, and reaching a height of 2–4". Illustration 93. *prostrata*, TH, a creeping or trailing miniature with variegated lvs. similar to those of *Ceropegia woodii*. *rubella*, TH, forms a small bush of red stems, and reddish, silver-veined lvs. Illustration 94. Culture: 1, 2, 3, 4, or 8; 10–11; 13; 15, 16 or 17—sometimes used for 18 with good results so long as the soil is not water-logged; 22 or 29. Propagation: 34. Uses: 39 or 42.

PERNETTYA (per NET ee uh). Ericaceae. *P. tasmanica*, HP, a mat-forming evergreen shrublet, 2–3", with dark green lvs., and white fls. followed by red berries. Culture: 3, 4, or 6; 9; 13; 16–17; 25 with addition of four parts acid peat moss. Propagation: 30. Uses: 41, 41a, or 42.

PETROCOSMEA (pet roh KOZ mee uh). Gesneriaceae. *P. kerrii*, TH, 4″ tall, 6″ in diameter, with hairy rosettes of quilted lvs. and pale lavender, violet-shaped fls. at any season the plant has warmth, bright light and humidity. Culture: 3, 4, or 8; 10–11; 14; 16, or 18; 22, 27, 28, or 29. Propagation: 33, or 36 of multiple crowns. Uses: 40 or 42.

*PHILODENDRON (fill oh DEN dron). Araceae. *P. sodiroi*, miniature in the juvenile stage; starve it, keeping the soil dry, put the plant in a humid place, and do not provide it with anything to climb on. Under this culture the silver-green, metallic, heart-shaped lvs. will remain small, slow-growing and miniature for an indefinite time. Culture: 3, 4, 7 or 8; 10–11; 12; 15, 16, 17 or 18; 21, 22, 24, 25, or 29. Propagation: 34. Uses: 37, 40, or 42.

PHLOX (flox). Polemoniaceae. *P. kelseyii*, HP, 3″, a dense, carpeting plant with light, glaucous lvs., and showy fls. of deep violet. 'Ronsdorf Beauty,' HP, 3″, a compact mound of lvs. with fls. of glowing salmon May-June. 'Star of Heaven,' HP, 3″, compact plants covered with rose fls. May-June. Culture: 4 or 6; 9; 13 winter, 14 other times; 16–17, except 19 in winter; 26. Propagation: 34 in July, or 36 in early spring. Uses: 41 or 42.

*PHOENIX (FEE nix). Palmae. *P. roebelenii*, the miniature date palm. As this palm comes from the greenhouse, it may be a seedling less than 10″ tall, but densely full of fronds, and delightful for a miniature garden, staying small for up to 5 years. Culture: 1, 2, 3, 4, 5, 6, or 7; 10–11; 13; 15, 16, or 17; 22, 24, 26, or 29. Propagation: 32. Uses: 39, 40, or 42.

PHYTEUMA (fye TEW muh). Campanulaceae. *P. comosum*, HP, 3–4″, blue fls. in July. *hemisphaericum*, HP, 3–4″, fls. of clear blue June-Sept. *serratum*, HP, 2–3″, with blue fls. in the summer. Culture: 6; 9 in winter; 13; 16; 22 with addition of some limestone chippings, and an annual early winter top--dressing of limestone, peat moss, flaked leaf mold, and chipped mortar. Propagation: 30, or 36 in the spring. Uses: 41 or 42.

PIERIS (PEER iss). Ericaceae. *P. nana*, HP, 3", tiny shrublet with white fls. in the summer. *japonica pygmaea*, HP, 10", a bushy shrublet with laciniated lvs. and new growth of bright bronze-pink. Culture: 4; 9 in winter; 13 in winter, 14 other times; 16–17; 22 deleting the garden soil. Propagation: 30. Uses: 39, 41, or 42. May be summered in shade outdoors.

PIMELEA (pye MEE lee uh). Thymelaeaceae. *P. coarctica*, HP, 4", a mat-forming shrublet covered with tiny gray lvs. and fragrant, small white fls. May-June, followed by white berries. Culture: 6; 9 in winter; 13; 16–17; 22, 24, or 26. Propagation: 32 or 34. Uses: 39, 41, or 42.

*PILEA (pye LEE uh). Urticaceae. *P. cadierei minima*, TH, 6", a miniature form of the popular aluminum plant; rosy

ILLUSTRATION 96. Pilea *depressa. (Scale: 4-inch pot.)*

ILLUSTRATION 97. Pilea *'Moon Valley.' (Scale: smaller leaves, 1 inch long.)*

stems, and quilted lvs. of grass-green and silver; branches freely, and with some pinching and trimming is easily kept under 6". *depressa*, TH, 1", a mat-forming trailing plant with succulent lvs. of bright, cool green. Illustration 96. *microphylla*, TH, the common artillery plant; trim and prune it to almost any size—easily kept under 8". 'Moon Valley' is a recent introduction. Pebbly leaves are brown and green; might easily be confused at first with the Iron Cross Begonia. Illustration 97. *nummulariifolia*, TH, similar to *depressa*, but not the same; leaves more round, slightly larger. *repens*, TH, a bushy little plant popularly known as the blackleaf panamiga; it has round, quilted, dark copper-brown lvs. and minute greenish white fls. Culture: 3, 4, 5, 6, 7 or 8; 10–11; 13–14; 16, 17 or 18; 22, 24, 26 or 29. Propagation: 34. Uses: 38 or 42.

*PLECTRANTHUS (plek TRANTH us). Labiatae. *P. coleiodes*, TH, has light green lvs. with margins of pure white, sometimes suffused with pink; these appear on a small coleus-like plant that may be pinched and cut back to any size desired. *P. hederacea*, TH, is a beautiful, easily-grown basket plant with heart-shaped lvs. of bright, fern-green, about half of their surface frosted with luminous silver. They are small— not more than 1" long, or wide at any point; scalloped margins. Pinch and shape plant to desired size. Culture: 3, 4, 5, 6, 7, or 8; 10–11; 13–14; 16–17; 22, 24, 26, 28, or 29. Propagation: 34. Uses: 38 for *hederacea*, 42 for both.

PODOCARPUS (poh doh KARP us). Taxaceae. *P. alpina*, HP, is a very slow-growing evergreen bushlet with dark green lvs. *totra halli*, HP, is a low- and slow-growing shrublet with yew-like foliage. Culture: 5, 6, or 7; 9–10; 13; 15–16; 22. Uses: 39 or 42.

*POLYSTICHUM (polly STITCH um). Polypodiaceae. *P. tsus-si-mense*, TH, 8", a dwarf fern that is particularly choice for planting in miniature landscapes inside a terrarium. It has small, leathery, dark green fronds. Culture: 1, 2, 3, 4, or 8; 10–11; 13; 16, 17, or 18; 22 or 29. Propagation: 36 in the spring. Uses: 40 or 42.

*PORTULACARIA (port yew lack AY ree uh). Portulaceae. *P. afra variegata*, TS, a small shrublet with reddish brown stems and close-set, small, opposite lvs. of gray-green in the center, broadly edged with, or sometimes entirely creamy white, the tiny margins finally rose-red. Commonly known as the rainbow bush. Culture: 5, 6, or 7; 10; 12; 15 or 16, but fresh air is important; 24 or 26. Propagation: 34. Uses: 39a or 42.

POTENTILLA (poh ten TILL uh). Rosaceae. *P. aurea*, HP, 4–6″, tuft-forming green lvs. and yellow fls. June-Aug.; var. *flore plena* has double yellow fls. *clusiana*, HP, 6″, has white fls. in June. *detommasii*, HP, 4″, has yellow fls. in the summer. *eriocarpa*, HP, 2″, has yellow fls. June-July. *nevadensis*, HP, 4″, has silky lvs. and yellow fls. in May. *nitida*, HP, 2″, has rose fls. June-July. *reptans flore plena*, HP, 4″, strong-growing trailer with double yellow fls. through most of the summer.

ILLUSTRATION 98. *Miniature plants from early herbals; all are in cultivation today.*

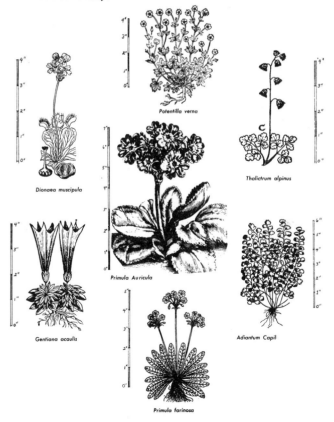

Potentilla verna

Thalictrum alpinus

Dionaea muscipula

Primula Auricula

Gentiana acaulis

Adiantum Capil

Primula farinosa

tonguei, HP, 3–6″, fls. of rich apricot with crimson spots July-Sept. (See Illustration 98.) *verna* var. *nana*, HP, 2″, a ground-hugging carpeter with yellow fls. in the summer. Culture: 6; 9–10; 13–14; 16–17; 26. Propagation: 33 at 55 to 65°, or 36 fall or spring. Uses: 39, 41, or 42.

PULMONARIA (pull moh NAY ree uh). Boraginaceae. *P. angustifolia*, HP, 3″, has March-May fls. of intense gentian-blue. *rubra*, HP, 3″, blooms March-May with fls. of orange-red. Culture: as for arabis, which see.

PRIMROSES, miniature, see under Primula.

PRIMULA (PRIM yew luh). Primulaceae. *P. allionii*, HP, 2″, pink fls. in the spring. *auricula* (Illustration 98), HP, 6–8″, variously colored fls. in the spring: var. *spectabilis*, HP, 2″, has fls. of bright rose-purple in early spring, and a rosette of marbled lvs. *bractworthii*, HP, 2–3″, striking large fls. in the spring from a ground-hugging rosette of lvs. *calycina*, HP, 4″, fls. of vibrant red in the spring. *carniolica*, HP, 4–6″, fragrant rose fls. in the spring. *clusiana*, HP, 5–6″, fls. of intense rose in the spring. *cottia*, HP, 4″, rose-pink fls. in the spring. *farinosa* (Illustration 98) HP, 4–6″, bird's-eye primrose; rose fls. in the spring. *glaucescens*, HP, 4–6″, blue fls. in the spring. *glutinosa*, HP, 4″, fragrant, purple fls. in the spring. *hirsuta*, HP, 4″, pink, lilac and white fls. in early spring. *integrifolia*, HP, 3″, reddish-lilac fls. in the spring. *Juliae*, HP, 2–3″, pink fls. in the spring. *marginata hyacinthina*, HP, 3–6″, lavender fls. in the spring. *Menziesiana*, HP, 4″, purple fls. in the spring. *minima*, HP, 1″, pink fls. in the spring. *pandora*, HP, 2″, large fls. above a ground-hugging rosette of lvs., in the spring. *pedemontana*, HP, 3″, pink fls. in the spring. *scotica*, HP, 1–2″, blue-purple fls. in the summer. *winteri*, HP, 3–6″, lavender or lilac fls. in the winter. Culture for *allionii, bractworthii, calycina, hirsuta, menziesiana, pandora* and *pedemontana:* 6; 9; 13–14; 16 except 19 in winter; 26 with addition of one part well-rotted cow manure. Propagation: 30 or 31, or 35 in spring after flowering, or in fall. Uses: 41 or 42. Culture for *auricula* and its varieties and *winteri:* 6; 9; 13-14; 16; 26 with addition of one part well-rotted cow manure. Propagation: 30 or 31, or 35 in spring after flowering or in fall. Uses: 41a or 42. Culture for *carniolica, clusiana, cottia, glaucescens, integrifolia, marginata hyacinthina,* and *minima:* 6; 9 in winter; 13–14; 16; 21 with addition of two parts peat moss. Propagation: 30 or 31, or 35 in spring after flowering, or in fall. Uses: 41 or 42. Culture for *farinosa, glutinosa, juliae* and *scotica:* 4; 9; 13–14; 16; 26 with addition of one part well-rotted cow manure. Propagation: 30 or 31, or 35 in spring after flowering, or in fall. Uses: 41 or 42.

*PTERIS (TARE iss). Polypodiaceae. *P. ensiformis evergemiensis,* TH, a miniature fern with silver and green fronds. *ensiformis victoriae* is similar, but showier; its silver lvs. are margined with deep green; it is small-growing and delicate in appearance. Culture: 1, 2, 3, 4, 5, 7, or 8; 10–11; 13; 16, 17, or 18; 22 or 29. Propagation: 36. Uses: 39, 40, or 42.

*PUNICA (PEW nick uh). Punicaceae. *P. granatum nana,* a miniature pomegranate with tan twigs that form a tree- or bushlike plant with narrow, willowy lvs. to 1 inch in length. These are a vibrant, bright shade of green, flushed along the edges with deep bronze. During the late winter, spring and summer it bears delicate-petaled fls. of vivid, glowing orange-red. 'Chico' is similar, but it has double flowers, and is sometimes called the carnation-flowered pomegranate. Both of these are among the finest of all house plants, and they may be pruned or pinched at any time to make bushier, more com-

ILLUSTRATION 99. Punica granatum nana, *the dwarf pomegranate. (Scale: "star" face of flower, 1 inch across.)*

pact specimens. Culture: 5, 6, 7, or 8; 10-11; 13; 15, 16 or 17; 22, 24, or 26. Propagation: 32, or 34 of half-ripened wood in summer. Uses: as a tree or bush for 39 or 42.

PUSCHKINIA (push KIN ee uh). Liliaceae. *P. scilloides*, 4″, a hardy bulb with blue, striped-white fls. in the spring. May be forced, as for the other hardy bulbs; see Chapter 5.

RAMONDA (ray MON duh). Gesneriaceae. *R. myconi*, syn. *pyrenaica*, HP, 5″, with rosettes of quilted, crinkled, dark green lvs. and violet fls. in May. *nathaliae*, HP, 4–6″, has fls. of intense lavender in June. *serbica*, HP, 4″, has lavender-lilac fls. May-June; var. *alba* is white-flowered. Culture: 2, 3. or 4; 9 in winter; 12–13; 16, except 19 in winter; 22. Propagation: 33, or by 34 (leaf cuttings), or 36 in summer. Uses: 39, 41a, or 42.

RAOULIA (ray OOH lee uh). Compositae. *R. australis*, HP, 1″, a minute mat-forming creeper with silvery lvs. Culture: 6; 9 in winter; 13; 19 in winter; 21. Propagation: 36 in the spring. Uses: 41 or 42. Mulch with small pebbles or chippings as the foliage does not like to rest on the soil.

*REBUTIA (ruh BEW tee uh). Cactaceae. *R. kupperiana*, TC, is a miniature cactus with glowing red fls. *minuscula*, TC, has bodies no larger than a good fat thumb, and is often hidden by its fiery-scarlet fls. Almost all rebutias are desirable for miniature gardens. They are easily grown from seeds; sow at 70° and fls. should come within two years. Culture as for mammillaria.

*RHIPSALIDOPSIS (rip sal ih DOP sis). Cactaceae. *R. rosea*, TC, a shrub-like small plant with fls. of rose-pink with an eye of more intense color. Culture: 3, 4, 5, 6, or 7; 10–11; 13; 15, 16, or 17; 25, or in fir bark. Propagation: 34. Uses: 38, 39, 39a or 42.

*RHIPSALIS (RIP sal iss). Cactaceae. *R. cereuscula*, TC, plant similar to hatiora, but with pink-white fls. *mesembryanthemoides*, also similar to hatiora, but with small white fls. *teres* is like *cereuscula*, but smaller. Culture: as for hatiora.

RHODODENDRON (roh doh DEN dron). Ericaceae. *R. myrtilloides*, syn. *R. campyloginum*, HP, 6″, a small shrub with dark, glossy lvs. and small, waxy fls. of plum-red in spring.

pemakoense, syn. *R. uniflorum, HP,* 8–10″, is a compact shrub with rose-pink fls. in early spring. Culture: 4 or 6; 9; 13–14; 16–17; 25 with addition of four parts peat moss. Propagation: 34 in late summer, and with bottom heat—a difficult feat. Uses: 39, 41, or 42.

'Gumpo' azalea is a dwarf rhododendron, more or less trailing shrublet with frilled, white fls. measuring up to 5″ in diameter. It is available also in a pink-flowered form. This azalea, along with others listed here, is an invaluable plant for the home greenhouse. Many hybrid azaleas, if bought as small rooted cuttings, can be pruned after flowering each year, and trained to stay indefinitely under 12″. For example: 'Hexe' is a late-flowering hybrid with compact growth and large fls. of intense crimson-red. 'Fiesta' makes a compact bush, covered with ruffled flowers of vivid red from midseason to late. 'Coral Bells' is low, free-branching, and has small, sometimes nearly bell-like fls. of bright pink. Culture: 3, 4, 5, 6, or 7; 9; 13–14; 16; 25. Uses: 39, 41, or 42.

RHODOHYPOXIS (roh doh hye POX iss). Amaryllidaceae. *R. baurii, HP,* 2–4″, a bulbous plant with narrow, grasslike lvs. and star-shaped fls. of carmine at intervals all through the summer. *platypetala,* 2″, has white or powder-pink fls. in early summer. Culture: 5, 6, or 7; 10–11; 13; 16; 21, 24 or 26. Propagation: 33, 36 in early spring. Uses: 39, 41, or 42.

ROMANZOFFIA (roh man ZOFF ee uh). Hydrophyllaceae. *R. sitchensis, HP,* 3–4″, white fls. in the spring. *suksdorfii, HP,* 2″, white fls. in the spring. *unalaschkensis, HP,* 3″, a saxifraga-like plant with white fls. Culture: 5 or 6; 9–10; 13; 16; 24 or 26. Propagation: 36 in spring. Uses: 39, 41, or 42.

ROMULEA (rom yew LEE uh). Iridaceae. *R. rosea, HHP,* 6″, a bulbous plant with yellow-throated carmine-red fls. in the spring. Culture: 5 or 6; 10–11; 13–14; 15–16; 22, with the addition of one teaspoon of bone meal to each 3-inch pot of soil. Propagation: 36 in the fall. Uses: 39, 41, or 42.

ROSCOEA (ross KOH ee uh). Zingiberaceae. *R. alpina, HP,* 6″, has showy fls. of purple-pink in the summer. Culture: 3, 4, 5, 6, 7, or 8; 10–11; 13; 16–17; 22, 26, or 29. Propagation: 32, or 36 in spring. Uses: 39, 41, or 42.

ROSES, miniature, see Chapter 10.

*ROSMARINUS (rose muh RYE nus). Labiatae. *R. officinalis* var. *prostratus*, HP, 6″, a low-growing rosemary with lavender fls. when the weather is warm and sunny. Culture: 5, 6, 7, or 8; 9–10; 12–13; 15–16; 22, 24, or 26. Propagation: 34 in early fall. Uses: 38 as hanging basket, or 42.

SAINTPAULIA, see miniature African violets, Chapter 3.

SALVIA (SAL vee uh). Labiatae. *S. officinalis tricolor*, HP, is a sage that can be kept trimmed to 8″ or less, though naturally it goes to 12 or more. The gray-green foliage is quilted and beautifully marked with white and pink; an excellent house plant. Culture: 5, 6, 7 or 8; 9–10; 12–13; 15–16; 22, 24, or 26. Propagation: 34 in early fall or in spring. Uses: 42.

SAXIFRAGA (sax IF ruh juh). Saxifragaceae. *S. allioni*, HP, 3″, a tuft of green lvs. with spring fls. of white. *apiculata*, HP, 4″, yellow fls. in spring; var. *alba*, white fls. *arco-valleyi*, HP, 1–2″, large fls. of rose-pink in March, or later. *ardense splendens*, HP, 3″, vivid carmine fls. in the spring. *atropurpurea*, HP, 1–3″, starry crimson fls. in the spring, *biasolettii*, HP, 3–4″, red fls. in the spring, and needs more sun than most others. *boydii*, HP, 3″, a tiny mat of lvs. with spring fls. of citron-yellow. *buseriana* 'His Majesty,' HP, 2″, a strikingly beautiful variety with large white fls. tinted pink and appearing Feb.-March. *buseriana magna*, HP, 3″, has large white fls. on crimson stems. *buseriana sulphurea*, HP, 2″, has powder-yellow fls. in early spring, rose-red stems and silver foliage. *cranbourne*, HP, 1–2″, large bright pink fls. March-April. *elizabethae*, HP, 3″, lvs. in mats of bright green with pale yellow fls. 'Faldonside,' HP, 2″, rosettes of gray-blue lvs. with citron-yellow fls. Feb. and March. 'Gloriana,' HP, 2″, has fls. of pale pink, *haagii*, HP, 2″, forms a spiny cushion of lvs. and sends up bright, golden fls. 'Hocker Edge,' HP, 1″, has rosettes of dark blue lvs. and pink fls. *jenkinsae*, HP, 2″, an outstanding hybrid with pink fls. Feb.-March. *juniperifolia*, HP, 3″, silver rosettes of long lvs. with fls. of soft pink to yellowish in the spring. 'Mother of Pearl,' HP, 2″, an early-flowering variety with fls. of pale pink. 'Myra,' HP, 1″, rosettes of silver-green lvs. with fls. of bright pink in

ILLUSTRATION 100. Saxifraga stolonifera tricolor, *the variegated strawberry-geranium, shown growing in a glass container with clear plastic covering the top to assure high humidity. (Scale: 4-inch container opening.)*

March, *petraschii*, HP, 3–4″, with white fls. in spring. *retusa*, HP, 1″, has prostrate, minute glossy lvs. with pink or red fls. in early summer. 'Riverslea,' HP, 2″, forms a cushion of silver lvs. and sends up crimson-purple fls. in March. *rocheliana*, HP, 4″, frosty green rosettes of lvs. with large white fls. *stolonifera*, HHP, the popular strawberry-geranium, forms a compact rosette when young, up to 12″ if allowed to mature. However, the baby plants are tiny, and outstanding for all types of miniature gardening for a considerable time after they are planted. This species bears white and pink fls. in spring and summer. *stolonifera tricolor* (see Illustration 100) sometimes sold as 'Magic Carpet,' is a magnificent plant with its lvs. of dark green heavily margined with creamy white, the outer edges of the white flushed with crimson. *stribrnyi*, HP, 4″, forms a large silver rosette of lvs. and sends up rose-purple stems of pink fls. in the summer. *suendermannii major*, HP, 3″, has rose-pink fls. borne on red stems. *valdensis*, HP, 1–3″, has white fls. in the summer and it needs sun. Culture: 3, 4, or 6 (*stolonifera* and vars. also 8); 9–10; 12–13; 16–17, but 19 in winter except *stolonifera;* compose growing medium of two parts garden soil, two parts leaf mold flaked or peat moss, and one part clean, sharp sand and one part grit (limestone chippings). Propagation: 34 in spring and rooted in sand. Uses: 38, 39, 41, 41a, or 42. It is not possible to generalize about the culture of saxifraga species for they have many individual and peculiar likes and dislikes. *Stolonifera* and its varieties are valuable house plants, of course, and widely obtainable. Certainly they are not difficult, but the others described here are truly wonderful plants that merit and demand special attention.

SCABIOSA (skay bee OH suh). Dipsaceae. *S. parnassii*, HP, 3″, has prostrate lvs. of blue, and sends up mauve-pink fls. in the summer. *scabra* is a miniature form of *S. caucasia*, HP, with growth just a few inches high and blooms through most of the summer; it needs the soil mixture described for the saxifragas. Culture: 6; 9 in winter, then 10; 13; 16; 24 with light annual top-dressing of well-rotted manure. Propagation: 32, or 36 in early spring. Uses: 39, 41 or 42.

*SCHIZOCENTRON (skee zoh CEN tron). Melastomaceae. *S. elegans*, syn. *Heeria elegans,* or *Heterocentron elegans,* is known popularly as the Spanish shawl plant. It is creeping or trailing, eventually forming a dense mat in the pot, then spilling off the sides in a beautiful cascade. The glowing rose-purple fls. are more than 1″ across, and they appear in the winter, spring and summer. Culture as for heterocentron.

*SCILLA (SILL uh). Liliaceae. *S. violacea,* a small bulbous plant to 8″ tall with spikes of delicate, airy white fls. The lvs. are strikingly leopard-spotted—deep green spots on a silver background. The undersides are flushed with glowing rosy wine color. It does not die down as do most scillas. Culture: 3, 4, 5, 6, 7, or 8; 9–10; 13; 16 or 17; 22, 24, 26, or 29. Propa-

ILLUSTRATION 101. Scilla violacea. *(Scale: 2-inch pot.)*

gation: 36 in the fall if the plant has any offsets. Uses: 39, 40, or 42. (Illustration 101.)

*SCINDAPSUS (sin DAP sus). Araceae. *S. pictus argyraeus*, TH, has creeping, cordate lvs. of blue-green. They are satiny. Culture: 3, 4 or 8; 10–11; 13; 15, 16, 17 or 18; 22 or 29. Propagation: 34 by layering. Uses: 38, 40, or 42.

*ŠEDUM (SEE dum). Crassulaceae. *S. alamosanum*, TS, 2″, pink fls. in the summer. *amecamecanum*, TS, 6″, apricot or orange fls. in the summer. *amplexicaule*, HP, 2″, a curious species that looks like dried oats during hot weather, but turns green upon the arrival of cool autumn days. *anglicum*, HP, 2″, evergreen lvs., and white fls., blushed pink, in the summer. *bellum*, TS, 3″, purple and white fls. in the summer. *brevifolium*, ½″, gray-blue lvs., and white flowers in the summer. *caeruleum*, HA, 2–3″, blue fls. in late summer. *cupressoides*, TS, 3″, late summer fls. of golden-yellow. *dasyphyllum*, HP, 1–2″, mat-forming of blue-gray, evergreen miniature rosettes, with white fls., the petal ends tinged pink, June-July. *gracile*, 2″, white fls. in summer, *gypsicolum*, 3″, white fls. in summer. *hirsutum*, 3″, pink or white fls. in summer. *hispanicum*, 2″ white fls. in summer. *hobsonii*, 1″, a deciduous species with pink fls. in summer. *humifusum*, TS, 2″, yellow fls. in spring. *jepsonii*, HP, a miniature with fleshy purple lvs. and sprays of golden fls. *lineare variegatum*, blue- or gray-green lvs. margined with cream-white, sometimes the white tinted with pink; ideal for 37 and 39a. *lydium*, 2″, white fls. in June. *moranense*, 4″, white fls. in summer; var. *arboreum*, 5–6″, takes on the form of a tiny tree. *oaxacanum*, TS, 2″, yellow fls. in summer. *pachyphyllum*, a miniature succulent with fat, spooned lvs. of light, powdery blue-green, the ends red-tipped; yellow fls. *pilosum*, HB, 3″, rosy red fls. in early summer. *spatulifolium purpureum*, HP, 3–4″, yellow fls. May-July. *spurium*, 2″, pink fls. in summer. *stahlii*, TS, 4″, lvs. set on small stems like beads, the ends tipped with red when grown in poor soil and full sunlight; fls. yellow in the fall. *tatarinowii*, 2–3″, has pink fls. in late summer. 'Waight Hybrid,' HP, 2″, has mealy, gray lvs., almost white, with yellow fls. Culture: 5, 6, or 7; 9, 10, or 11; 13

ILLUSTRATION 102.
Selaginella kraussiana
brownii.

when in active growth, then very little; 15–16; 24 with addition of one part well-rotted cow manure. Propagation: 32 at
55–65°, 34 in summer or 36. Uses: 37, 38, 39a, or 42.

*SELAGINELLA (sell aj ih NELL uh). Selaginellaceae. *S. kraussiana
brownii*, TH, 1″, a creeping, moss-like plant with fine-cut lvs.
of brightest, grass green; sometimes known as Irish moss.
(Illustration 102 & 103) *martensii variegata*, TH, is more
upright growing than *brownii*, and its lacy foliage is
splashed with areas of cream-white. *uncinata*, TH, is a
ground-hugging creeper with lvs. of peacock blue. Culture: 1,
2, 3, 4, or 8; 9, 10 or 11; 13–14; 16, 17 or 18; 22, 27, or 29.
Propagation: 34. Uses: 40 or 42.

SHORTIA (SHORT ee uh). Diapensiaceae. *S. soldanelloides*, syn.
Schizocodon soldanelloides, HP, 4–5″, has glossy, round lvs.
that change from bright green to bronze in the fall, and
bell flowers fringed along the edges and of glowing pink
color. *galacifolia*, TH, 3–6″, is another species that should
be cultivated more in containers. It has white fls. in early
spring. Culture: 4 or 6; 13; 16; 25 with the addition of four
parts peat moss. Propagation: 36 in the spring. Uses: 39, 41,
or 42.

*SIDERASIS (sye DARE uh sis). Commelinaceae. *S. fuscata*, TH,
has stemless lvs. of reddish brown, velvety plush. In the
spring it bears bright blue fls. an inch across. As a young
plant, this is an excellent miniature. Culture: 3, 4, 5, 6, 7, or
8; 10–11; 13; 16, 17 or 18; 24, 26, or 29. Propagation: 36. Uses:
39, 40, or 42.

SILENE (sye LEEN ee). Caryophyllaceae. *S. acaulis pedicularis,* HP, 2″, has rose-pink fls. borne well above the foliage through most of the summer. *acaulis salmon,* as sold by Alpenglow Gardens, HP, 2″, has a mat of green lvs. and delicate salmon fls. through most of the summer. Culture: 6; 9 in winter, 10–11 other times; 13; 16; grow in equal parts loam, peat moss, and coarse sand or pebbles. Propagation: 31, or 36 in the spring. Uses: 39, 41, or 42.

SINNINGIA PUSILLA, the miniature gloxinia, see Chapter 2.

SISYRINCHIUM (siss ee RINK ee um). Iridaceae. *S. brachypus,* HP, 6″, has grass-like lvs. and fls. of yellow through most of

ILLUSTRATION 103. Selaginella kraussiana *growing in a glass bowl with clear glass covering to assure high humidity. (Scale: bowl opening 6 inches across.)*

ILLUSTRATION 104. Selaginella emmeliana. *(Scale: 2-inch pot.)*

the summer. Culture: 5 or 6; 10–11; 13; 16; 22. Propagation: 33, or 36 in the spring. Uses: 39, 41, or 42.

SOLDANELLA (soul duh NELL uh). Primulaceae. *S. alpina*, HP, ¾–3″, blue-purple fls. from March to May. *ganderi*, HP, 2″, fls. of delicate lilac in March. *minima*, HP, 2″, lavender and purple fls. in April, *neglecta*, HP, 3″, lilac fls. in spring. *pindicola*, HP, 3″ lavender fls. in the spring. *pusilla*, HP, 2–4″, fls. of delicate lavender-lilac in April. Culture: 6; 9–10; 13; 16, except 19 during the fall and winter; 21 with some limestone chippings. Propagation: 31, or 36 in spring. Uses: 41 or 42.

SOLIDAGO (soh lih DAY go). Compositae. *S. brachystachys*, HP, 6″, a miniature goldenrod with a profusion of golden-yellow fls. from Aug. to Oct. Culture: 5 or 6; 9 in winter, then 10–11; 13–14; 15–16; 26. Propagation: 31, or 36 spring or fall. Uses: 39 or 42.

SONERILA (sohn ehr ILL uh). Melastomaceae. *S. margaritacea*, TH, a small begonia-like plant with red stems, and copper-green lvs. that are tinted rosy purple from beneath; it has fls. of lavender-rose; var. *argentea* has silver-white lvs. and a distinct network of dark green veins; var. *hendersonii* has coppery maroon lvs. that are densely patterned with spots of silver-white, with undersides of rosy purple; var. 'Mme. Baextele' is a miniature, similar to the type, but with lvs. of silver-white with green veins and undersides of rosy purple. Culture: 3, 4, 5, 6, 7, or 8; 10–11; 13; 16; 17 or 18; 22 or 29. Propagation: 34. Uses: 40 or 42.

*SPATHICARPAS (spath ick ARP us). Araceae. *S. sagittifolia*, TH, has miniature lvs. like a calla lily (zantedeschia), and a most unusual fl., insignificant to most, but appreciated by any avid indoor gardener. The buds appear from the base of the plant as if they were new leaves, but they unfold and recurve slightly to reveal a ridge of shiny white bead-like fls. Culture: 3, 4, 5, 6, or 8; 11; 13–14; 16, 17 or 18; 22, 26, 29. Propagation: 33, or 36. Uses: 40 or 42.

SPIRAEA (spye REE uh). Rosaceae. *S. decumbens*, HP, 3–8″, fls. in May or June, borne in loose clusters about 1½ inches in diameter. *digitata nana*, HP, 9″, bears large heads of rose-red fls. from August to Oct. *hacquetii*, HP, 4″, grows as a miniature shrub with downy stems and lvs. and fluffy white fls. from June to Aug. Culture: 5 or 6; 9 in winter, then 10; 13-14; 16-17; 24 or 26. Propagation: 34 in summer, or remove offshoots in the fall. Uses: 39, 41, or 42, *hacquetii* and *decumbens* may be pruned at the end of their flowering period; remove straggly or weak wood. *Digitata nana* may be pruned back severely in late winter or early spring. These plants benefit from having the flower clusters removed as soon as they begin to fade.

STACHYS (STACK iss). Labiatae. *S. corsica*, HP, 2″, a carpeting plant with pink and cream fls. in the summer. *lavandulaefolia*, HP, 6″, has gray, velvety lvs. and purple-red fls. June-Aug. Culture: 6; 9 in winter; 13; 16; 24. Propagation: 32, or 36 spring or fall. Uses: 39 or 42.

*STENANDRIUM (stuh NAN dree um). Acanthaceae. *S. lindenii*, TH, 6–10″, with lvs. of dark green suffused with bright chartreuse to golden vein-work. *Chamaeranthemum igneum* (described in this chapter) is very similar, and the two plants together make a fetching couple. Culture: 3, 4, 5, 6, 7, or 8; 10–11; 13–14; 16, 17, or 18; 22 or 29. Propagation: 34. Uses: 38, 40, or 42.

STREPTOCARPUS (strep toh KAR pus). Gesneriaceae. *S. rimicola* is a miniature with myriads of small white blooms. Grower Michael Kartuz advises that faded flowers be kept picked to prolong flowering. *saxorum*, TH, has succulent, rounded, opposite, sometimes whorled lvs., and white-throated, lavender-blue fls. over a long period of time—in fact, whenever the plant is making active growth, is receiving sunlight for part of the day (or fluorescent light), warmth and humidity it will have flowers. Although *saxorum* eventually makes a large plant, here is how to have small flowering ones: Insert tip cuttings, preferably that show flower buds, in moist peat moss and sand, or in growing mediums 27, 28, or 29. Provide with warmth and high humidity, and they will not only form roots, but the buds will continue to develop and provide many weeks of bloom without exceeding 8″ in height. Culture: 3, 4, 5, 6, 7, or 8; 10–11; 13–14; 16, 17 or 18; 22, 27, 28 or 29. Propagation: 33, or 34. Uses: 38, or for 42 while young.

ILLUSTRATION 105. Syngonium podophyllum '*Imperial White.*'

*SYNGONIUM (sin GO nee um). Araceae. *S. podophyllum* 'Imperial White,' TH, a beautiful foliage plant that is easily
grown, and stays under 8" for an indefinite time while it is
in the juvenile state (that is, before it starts to climb). Culture: 3, 4 or 8; 10–11; 13–14; 15, 16, 17 or 18; 22, 27 or 29.
Propagation: 36. Uses: 39, 40 or 42. (Illustration 105.)
TAGETES (tuh JEE teez). Compositae. (Miniature or Dwarf-
Growing Marigolds.) *T. patula nana* 'Dainty Marietta,' HHA,
6", typical marigold foliage, and single fls. of yellow with
mahogany blotch; var. 'Helen Chapman,' HHA, 6", has fls. of
bright gold with a small red area near the petal bases; var.
'Primrose,' HHA, 6", has double fls. of glowing yellow, the
centers slightly curled; var. 'Sunny,' HHA, 3", has single,
yellow fls. *signata pumila* 'Gnome,' HHA, 6", has fls. of deep
orange; var. 'Lulu,' HHA, 6", is completely compact and becomes smothered in ¾" single fls. of intense, sunny yellow.
Culture: 5 or 6; 9–10 in winter; 13; 16 or 17; 26. Propagation: 33. Uses: 39 or 42.
TECOPHILAEA (tay kok fill EE uh). Amaryllidaceae. *T. cyanocro-
cus leichtlinii*, HP, 3", a bulbous plant with spring fls. of
powder blue, the centers glistening white. Culture: 5 or 6;
9 in winter; 13, except dry during summer; 15–16; 23 with
addition of one part well-rotted cow manure. Propagation:
36, at time of repotting in late summer or early fall. Uses:
39, 41, or 42.

TEUCRIUM (TEW kree um). Labiatae. *T. polium*, HP, 4", a gray-leaved shrublet with yellow fls. in the summer; it is cultivated not only for its fls. but for its overall form and coloring. *subspinosum*, HP, 3", is similar to *polium*, but has lilac-pink fls. in Aug., and the bushlet is spiny. Culture: as for stachys.

THALICTRUM (thuh LICK trum). Ranunculaceae. *T. alpinus*, HP, 4–6", yellow-green fls. in the summer. *chelidonii*, HP, 6", has fls. of lilac-rose in the summer. *kiusianum*, HP, 4–6", a beautiful little perennial with ferny lvs. and long-lasting fls. of intense rose-mauve. Culture: 4 or 6; 9 in winter; 13; 16; 25. Propagation: 36 in early spring. Uses: 39, 41a, or 42.

THLASPI (th LASS pee). Cruciferae. *T. alpinum*, HP, 3–4", has rosettes of shiny green lvs. and spikes of white fls. *bellidifolium*, HP, 2–3", has rosy purple fls. in the summer. *rotundifolium*, HP, 2–3", has fls. of rose-lilac in the summer. Culture: 6; 9 in winter; 13; 15–16; 24 or 26. Propagation: 31 or 32, 36 in fall or spring. Uses: 39, 41, or 42.

THYMUS (TIME us). Labiatae. Thyme. *T. citriodorus aureus*, HP, 2", carpeting plant with lemon-scented, golden lvs. *doerfleri minus*, HP, 2", a creeping plant with hairy, white stems and purple-red fls. in the summer. *ericaefolius*, HP, 4", forms a globular little bush of bronzed, golden foliage covered with red fls. in the summer. *Herba-barona*, HP, 3", is a carpeting plant with caraway-scented fls. of purple color. *membranaceus*, HP, 4", has white bracts in the summer. *serpyllum coccineus*, HP, 2", a creeping plant with crimson-red fls.; var. *minor*, HP, 2", is tuft-forming with tiny small lvs. of green and red fls. in the summer. *serpyllum lanuginosus*, HP, 2", is known popularly as the wooly thyme because of its carpet-like growth of wooly, gray lvs. It has pink fls. in July. Culture: 5 or 6; 9 in winter; 12–13; 15–16; 21. Propagation: 31 or 32, 34, or 35 in the spring. Uses: 38, 39, 41, or 42.

*TILLANDSIA (till AND see uh). Bromeliaceae. *T. ionantha*, TH, 2", a choice miniature that measures less than 2 by 2 inches at maturity. It is closely related to Spanish moss—*Tillandsia usneoides*—and belongs to the pineapple family.

ILLUSTRATION 106. Tillandsia ionantha, *a miniature bromeliad. (Scale: 2-inch pot.)*

Ionantha grows in a loose rosette of gray-green lvs. which, at flowering time, are suffused with bright pink. The tubular fls. of purple-blue appear at the center of the rosette. The bright yellow anthers extend beyond the end of the flower tube. Michael Kartuz recommends handling this plant in a very small pot of osmunda fiber, and growing it in full sunlight. He suggests further that the plant be given moisture by pouring water in the center of the urn-shaped rosette. Culture: 1, 2, 3, 4, 5, 6, 7, or 8; 10–11; 13; 16–17; 22, or in very small pot of osmunda fiber. Propagation: 36. Uses: 37, 39a, or 42. (Illustration 106.)

*TOMATO. Solanaceae. Three midget tomatoes, all bearing clusters of cherry-like edible fruits, qualify for inclusion here —the only vegetables small enough to be listed: 'Puck,' a variety from Webbs of England, 'Tiny Tim,' of the Farmer Seed and Nursery Company, Faribault, Minnesota, and 'Tom Tit,' from Reads of England are recommended for a sunny, warm window garden, for under fluorescent lights, and most of all for a sunny, warm greenhouse. Culture: 5, 6, 7, or 8; 10–11; 13; 16; 26 with the addition of one part well-rotted cow manure. Propagation: 33. Uses: 42. Discard after heavy fruiting. Jarring a plant in bloom will help to effect pollination; or use one of the fruitsetting hormone sprays.

TORENIA (toh REEN ee uh). Scrophulariaceae. *T. fournieri grandiflora nana compacta* 'Gefion,' is a miniature, usually shorter, in fact, than its name. It is excellent for pots, and although it normally blooms all summer and into the fall, it may be forced in a sunny, cool greenhouse, or in a sunny, moist window garden; also grown successfully under fluorescent lights. Culture: 5, 6, 7, or 8; 9–10; 13; 16–17; 26. Propagation: 32. Uses: 38, 39, or 42. Pinch seedlings at least twice to induce compactness.

*TRADESCANTIA (trad es KANT ee uh). Commelinaceae. *T. multiflora*, a miniature form of common wandering Jew, TH, a creeping plant with small dark lvs. and insignificant white fls. *navicularis*, TH, is a much showier miniature with chainlike or plaited lvs. of boat shape, and copper-green in color, rosy-purple beneath. Culture: 5 or 6 for *navicularis;* 3, 4, 5, 6, 7, or 8 for *multiflora;* 10–11; 13; 15–16; 24 or 26. Propagation: 34. Uses: 38.

*TRIFOLIUM (trye FOH lee um). Leguminosae. *T. alpinum*, HP, 4″, is a clover with light pink fls. in the summer. *uniflorum*, HP, 2″, has fls. of dark pink in the summer. Culture: 5 or 6; 9 in winter, then 10–11; 12–13; 15, 16 or 17; 26. Propagation: 36 in spring or fall. Uses: 39 or 42.

VALERIANA (vuh leer ee AY nuh). Valerianaceae. *V. arizonica*, HP, 2–6″, cheerful fls. of bright pink in March. *montana*, HP, 2–6″, has clusters of pure pink fls. in the summer. Culture: 6; 9 in winter, then 10–11; 13; 16–17; 26. Propagation: 31–32, or 36 in early spring. Uses: 39, 41, or 42.

VERONICA (vuh RON ick uh). Scrophulariaceae. *V. allionii*, HP, 2″, lavender-blue fls. in June and July. *armena*, HP, 3″, a creeping or trailing plant with fls. of brilliant, gentian blue. *caespitosa*, HP, 1–2″, has pink fls. May and June. *cinerea*, HP, 2–4″, with pink fls. July and Aug. *filiformis*, HP, 1–3″, a carpet-forming plant that smothers itself with blue fls. in the spring and summer. *guthriana*, HP, 6″, a miniature bushlet with evergreen foliage and fls. of intense, deep blue. *pageana*, HP, 6″, a miniature shrublet with silver-green, glaucous lvs. and fls. of lilac in early summer. *pectinata rosea*, HP, 3″, is a trailing plant with gray-green lvs. and rose-pink fls. May and

June. *repens*, HP, 1–3″, forms a mat of green lvs. and has flowers of white to pale blue from June to Aug. *rupestris nana rosea*, HP, 3″, is a miniature trailing plant that bears spikes of rose-pink fls. from May to July. Culture: 6; 9 in winter; 13; 16–17; 26 with addition of half part well-rotted cow manure. Propagation: 31, or 36 in spring or fall. Uses: 38, 39, 41, or 42.

VIOLA (vye OH luh). Violaceae. *V. alpina*, HP, 3″, with purple fls. in May. *arenaria rosea*, HP, 3″, a tuft-forming plant with fls. of bright pink during May and June. *biflora*, HP, 3″, has twin flowers of yellow to each stem in June. *hederacea*, HP, 2–3″, a mat-forming plant with creeping stems set with ivy-like lvs. and lavender and white fls. May-Sept. *nana compacta*, HP, ½″, has wee mounds of dark green lvs. and carmine-striped white fls.; this one is a dandy! *pinnata*, HP, 2–3″, has rosy lavender fls. in May and June. Culture: 5–6; 9 in winter, then 10; 13 in winter, then 14; 16–17; 26 with addition of a half part well-rotted cow manure. Propagation: 31 in spring or late summer, or 36 in early fall. Uses: 39, 41, or 42.

WAHLENBERGIA (wall en BERG ee uh). Campanulaceae. *W. tasmanica*, HP, 3″, has bell flowers of blue from June to August. Culture: 6; 9 in winter; 13; 16–17, except 19 in winter; 25. Propagation: 33, 34 in summer, or 36 in the spring. Uses: 39, 41, or 42.

ILLUSTRATION 107. *Highly fragrant, double-flowered English violet (species of* Viola*). (Scale: 3-inch pot.)*

🌿 CULTURAL GUIDE FOR MINIATURE PLANTS

THE CODE	
TO CULTURE	READING THE CODE

Light Requirement

1   North window with bright light all day, or east, south or west window that is shaded by a building, tree or shrub.

2   Shaded location in greenhouse, as underneath a bench, where light is constant, but not as bright as on top of the bench in a shaded greenhouse.

3   East window that receives morning sunlight and bright light the rest of the day.

4   Evenly shaded greenhouse that receives some sunlight in the winter, but only bright daylight the rest of the year.

5   South window that receives full sunlight during fall, winter and early spring, shaded to some extent in summer, as by a deciduous tree or a thin curtain.

6   Greenhouse with sunlight most of the day in fall, winter and early spring, but shaded during late spring, summer and early fall. Particularly when growing alpine plants, shade is best provided by laths spaced 1″ apart on frames, and running north and south so that the sun does not remain on one part of the plant for very long at a time.

7   West window that receives full sunlight during the fall, winter and early spring, but shaded to some extent in the summer, as by a deciduous tree or a thin curtain.

8   Fluorescent-light culture suits this plant. Basic set-up is this: two, preferably three, 40-watt daylight tubes (or one or two daylight tubes with one deluxe warm

white) in a standard commercial reflector, 13 or 15″ wide, suspended 18″ from the surface of a bench 24 by 48″. Burn the lights 14 to 16 hours out of every 24, turning them on in the morning, off at bedtime.

Temperature Requirement

9   Cool—35 to 60 degrees F., as in a cold or cool greenhouse, sun-heated pit greenhouse, cold frame or a window garden in a room not occupied by people (except for taking care of and admiring the plant). Plants requiring this temperature, under good culture, tolerate much more warmth in summer—but proper shading and ventilation are all-important.

10   Moderate warmth—ranging from 60 to 72 degrees, F.; tolerant of more heat if the atmosphere is moist.

11   Warmth—ranging from 62 to 85 degrees F.

Moisture Requirement in the Soil

12   On the dry side—allow to be quite dry between waterings, but when watered, should be thoroughly moistened; then not again until the plant is dry. Under no circumstances should the base of the pot be left standing in a saucer of water.

13   Moderately moist soil—sometimes expressed as just nicely moist. Not fatal if it dries out occasionally, but better if it doesn't dry to the point of wilting the plant.

14   Growing medium that is constantly moist—wet at the immediate time of application of moisture, but changing to moderately moist before more water is applied. Drying out severely at any time harms the plant considerably.

THE CODE
TO CULTURE   READING THE CODE

Moisture Requirement in the Atmosphere

15   Less than 40 per cent relative humidity, as in the average house or apartment.

16   40 to 60 per cent relative humidity—average greenhouse atmosphere, or that of a humidified house or apartment, or unusually moist window garden.

17   High humidity, as in a humidified greenhouse—55 per cent relative humidity at all times, but in air that is freshened by circulation.

18   High humidity, as in a closed greenhouse, Wardian case or terrarium where ventilation is slight.

19   This plant is an alpine. Needs a dry, cool atmosphere in the winter.

Growing Medium

20 *   One part clean, sharp sand to one part garden soil.

21 *   One part loam, one part leaf mold, two parts sand.

22 *   Equal parts garden soil, leaf mold, peat moss and clean, sharp sand.

23 *   Three parts clean, sharp sand to one part flaked leaf mold.

24 *   Equal parts garden soil, leaf mold and sand.

25 *   Four parts leaf mold, one part garden soil and one part clean, sharp sand.

26 *   Two parts garden soil, one part leaf mold and one part clean, sharp sand.

27 **   75 per cent screened sphagnum moss, 25 per cent Perl-Lome (fine-textured form of horticultural perlite).

THE CODE	
TO CULTURE	READING THE CODE

28 ** One part coarse peat moss to one part coarse vermiculite.

29 ** Black Magic Planter or African Violet Mix, nationally distributed growing mediums by Parks-Barnes, Inc., available locally or by mail in quantities of one pound to a hundred, and useful for growing most potted plants, particularly those so keyed in this chapter. Or, use the G-B-S Mix, described in Chapter 2.

Propagation

30   By seeds sown in late fall or during the winter in a cold frame, preferably where snow can fall on the seedbed, and where seeds can be stratified by alternate freezing and thawing. A much quicker way is to utilize the freezing unit of a refrigerator or a deep freeze; freeze and thaw the seeds alternately, leaving them in the cold for a week or two, then in warmth for a day, then back in the cold. After this is repeated two or three times, chances for germination are good as soon as warmth and light are provided.

31   By seeds sown in early spring in a cool place.

32   By seeds sown in early spring warmth.

33   By seeds sown in warmth at any season in house or greenhouse.

34   By cuttings when the plant is in active growth, or as specified in the description of the individual plant.

35   By division, immediately after flowering.

36   By division, any time, or as specified in the description of the individual plant.

THE CODE
TO CULTURE   READING THE CODE

Suggested Uses (The planting of miniature gardens is included in Chapter 12.)

37   May be maintained for considerable time in a thumb-size plastic or clay pot (1¼ to 2″ size).

38   For hanging basket, or pot set on a pedestal.

39   For miniature garden in air that circulates freely.

39a   Same as 39 but for cacti and succulents.

40   For miniature garden in high humidity, as inside a terrarium or Wardian case.

41   For miniature trough garden in a cool, sunny greenhouse or sun-heated pit.

41a   Same as 41 except shaded.

42   Grow in regular plastic or clay pot.

---

* When the plants growing in these are in active growth, plant food may be necessary. Over-feeding will kill them quickly, and a fertilizer with high nitrogen content may promote lush leaf growth at the expense of flowers and the loss of miniature proportions. An organic fertilizer, such as fish emulsion, applied at half-strength is a safe way to provide food. With the alpine plants, be extremely careful about fertilizing, and do so only after study.

** With sterile mediums such as these, it is necessary that plants be fed with liquid fertilizer when they are in active growth. An analysis such as nitrogen 23, phosphorus 21, potash 17 produces a well-balanced diet for the production of foliage, flowers and roots. A ratio similar to 5-10-5 or 15-30-15 promotes flowering. Follow container directions explicitly; if you veer from them, do so toward *under-* not *over-feeding.*

12. Gardening with Miniature Plants

Growing miniature plants in tiny containers is the height of Lilliputian gardening. It is possible to have living, thriving, even flowering plants in dollhouse dishes, caps of toothpaste tubes, 1¼-inch plastic pots, in bottle lids and even in thimbles. If you like to pamper plants, here is your opportunity; the soil in thumb-size containers dries out quickly. Check it in the morning, at noon if possible, and again in the evening. Soil that is nicely damp in the morning may be parched by nightfall. Apply water with an eyedropper or, when possible, by immersing the pot until the growing medium and roots are moistened.

GARDENING IN THIMBLE-SIZE CONTAINERS

When you plant a thimble-size container, leave ⅛ inch of space at the top to allow room for watering. Some growers place a little bit of sand in the bottom of thimble-like pots, but I have not found this necessary; the problem is keeping the soil uniformly moist at all times, not keeping it drier.

Use fine-textured soil, and once every 7 to 14 days apply a few drops of very dilute (one-fourth-strength or less) liquid

ILLUSTRATION 108. *A window garden of miniature plants in thimble-size containers. Top row, left to right:* Ceropegia woodii, Acorus gramineus variegatus, Monanthes polyphylla, Acorus *and* Monanthes muralis. *Bottom row, left to right: tip cutting of* Kalanchoe fedtshenkoi variegata, Sinningia pusilla *in 1¼-inch pot,* Ficus repens pumila, *species of* Rebutia *and 'Needlepoint' English ivy.*

house-plant fertilizer. If the plants quickly outgrow their tiny containers, you may be feeding them too much. Also, in order to keep some of them to the right proportions, careful pinching or pruning is necessary. For example, a seed of an orange or lemon planted in a thimble may, without transplanting, be grown in it for up to three years.

Besides the miniature plants suggested below for these smallest of containers, the seedlings of most cacti and other succulents are delightful for this form of gardening. They have interesting shapes, unusual textures, appealing colors, and most of them tolerate or thrive in considerable drouth and heat.

ILLUSTRATION 109. *Ordinary fish bowl converts easily to a mini greenhouse for tiny plants. Front row, three kinds of miniature gloxinias. Back row, left to right:* Selaginella kraussiana brownii, *maidenhair fern and* Gesneria saxatilis.

ILLUSTRATION 110. *Contemporary ceramic container for a sunny patio holds a collection of succulents; it measures 24 inches long. Plants include various echeverias, crassulas, aeoniums, sedums and sempervivums. Photograph by Peart.*

🌿 A SELECTION OF THIMBLE-SIZE PLANTS

NAME	CULTURE
Acorus gramineus pusillus	See Chapter 11.
Ceropegia woodii	See Chapter 11; insert and root tip cutting in tiny container.
Conophytum species	See Chapter 11.
Ficus repens pumila	See Chapter 11.
Hedera helix varieties (English ivy)	See Chapter 8; root ½ to 1″ long tip cuttings of true miniatures like 'Needlepoint.'
Kalanchoe 'Tom Thumb,' and similar varieties	See Chapter 11; root budded tip cuttings 1″ long.
Kalanchoe fedtschenkoi variegata	Root the pink, cream and blue-green plantlets that form in the leaf axils and flower branches of older plants.
Lobularia maritima (sweet alyssum)	See Chapter 11; plant one or two seeds in tiny container; provide moisture and full sunlight. Pinch out growing tip to encourage ompactness; discard after flowering.
Monanthes muralis and *M. polyphylla*	See Chapter 11.
Philodendron sodiroi	See Chapter 11.
Sedum, various species	See Chapter 11; use seedling or tiny offset.
Sinningia pusilla (miniature gloxinia)	See Chapter 2.
Tillandsia ionantha	See Chapter 11; use tiny offset.

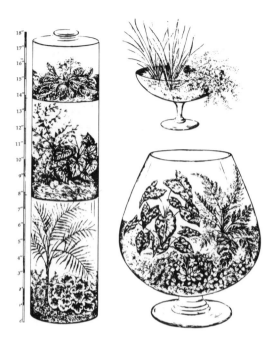

ILLUSTRATION 111. *Miniature plants in crystal containers.*

🌿 GARDENS IN CRYSTAL CONTAINERS

Many miniature plants are at their best when grown inside a crystal container. The plantings in Illustration 111 show some of these. The stacked candy jars contain, from top to bottom, *Saintpaulia* (African violet) variety 'Sweet Sixteen,' maidenhair fern (*Adiantum tenerum wrightii*), Begonia 'It,' a seedling of miniature palm (*Chamaedorea elegans 'bella'*) and *Saxifraga stolonifera tricolor*. The planting medium of the bottom jar is covered with *Selaginella kraussiana*. The sherbet dish contains *Acorus gramineus pusillus* on the left, and baby's-tears (*Helxine soleirolii*). The brandy snifter contains *Caladium humboldtii*, miniature fern (*Polystichum tsus-simense*), and a jewel-like focal point of *Sinningia pusilla* in bloom; the soil surface is covered by *Ficus pumila minima*.

Other plants for crystal containers include the African violets in Chapter 3, many begonia varieties (as indicated with individual descriptions in Chapter 4), the ivies in Chapter 8, the orchids in Chapter 9, and the plants in Chapter 11 which are suggested for use number 40.

How To Plant

When a glass container is used for growing plants, it is usually called a terrarium. Pieces of crystal, inexpensive globe-shaped fish tanks and rectangular aquariums make excellent terrariums. Just as in landscaping the outdoor garden, the first step with a terrarium is to do the gardening; that is, to shape the general contour of the soil in which the plants will be placed.

Several packaged growing mediums are available at local garden counters, and also by mail, that are satisfactory for terrariums. These include Black Magic African Violet Mix and the G-B-S Mix described in Chapter 2. Do not attempt to use a terrarium planting medium until it has been thoroughly moistened. When you have decided on the terrarium, put the plants in their places. Remove each from its container and gently insert and spread the roots into the soil. After planting is completed, use a clothes sprinkler or atomizer to water the plants in, and to wash pieces of the growing medium off the leaves and sides of the container.

Terrarium Maintenance

After planting, do not water a terrarium again until the soil at the top is beginning to show signs of dryness. Try to keep the medium nicely moist at all times. Too much water may cause roots to rot, and a lack of moisture may prevent them from growing. If the atmosphere is exceedingly dry, cover the opening of the terrarium with a piece of clear glass. This is usually left on only during the day and removed at night, or vice-versa, so that the plants have some fresh air.

To keep the terrarium in show condition, it is necessary to use a scissors from time to time to prune and clip the plants to desired size. Ficus, selaginella and helxine, in particular, outgrow their allotted space, and should be thinned before they run rampant.

🦅 MINIATURE LANDSCAPES

Most of the plants described in this book may be used to create exciting miniature landscapes. Such a planting could be your interpretation of the desert, a woodland dell, a formal rose garden or a bit of the Alps portrayed by tiny alpine plants. The basic requirement is to use plants together that grow well under the same conditions. That is, group cacti and other succulents, alpine plants, those that require shadiness, and so forth. In the Code of Culture, Chapter 11, the number 39 is used to indicate a plant that is suitable for a miniature garden in air that circulates freely. "Circulates freely" sets this garden apart from the terrariums and gardens in crystal containers. Number 39a follows 39 and indicates the same conditions, except drier and sunnier to suit most cacti and other succulents. The number 41 indicates a plant suitable for a miniature trough garden that is to be wintered in a cool, sunny (shady for 41a) greenhouse, or sun-heated pit. In the summer it can be either indoors or outside.

🦅 Desert Landscapes (Illustration 112)

Most plantings of cacti and succulents need abundant sunlight, warmth and a sandy, gritty planting medium. Plain containers, particularly those of pottery, are desirable for this kind of miniature landscape. Maintenance consists of applying moisture as needed by the species and varieties being

3"

2'

1."

0

LEFT TO RIGHT:
SEDUM DASYPHYLLUM
CRASSULA SCHMIDTII
ASTROPHYTUM MYRIOSTIGMA
CRASSULA TERES

HOUGHTON'S BRYOPHYLLUM
MONANTHES POLYPHYLLA
GASTERIA LILIPUTANA

ADROMISCHUS MACULATUS
RHIPSALIS MESEMBRYANTHEMOIDES
PORTULACARIA AFRA 'VARIEGATA'

ILLUSTRATION 112. *Miniature plants in desert landscapes.*

cultivated. Be watchful for insect invasions. The cottony mealybug is likely to attack at one time or another. Use a house-plant spray to control them.

It should not be necessary to replant a desert landscape more often than once every two years; perhaps even less frequently. Give the plants individual attention even though they are growing in a garden.

ILLUSTRATION 113. *Miniature woodland garden.*

🌿 A Miniature Woodland Garden (Illustration 113)

A woodland garden with stepping-stone paths winding and disappearing behind trees, shrubs and rocks inspired the dish garden shown in Illustration 113. A leak-proof baking pan fits snuggly inside the wicker basket. Brick-colored mosaic tiles form the path of miniature stepping stones. This same planter could have been planned as a formal garden with fine-bladed grass clipped close in the center and miniature plants around the edges. Or, think how delightful it would be to create a miniature perennial garden, designed in the style of England's best! For such a garden, you could use small mosaic tiles down the center to form a path with a miniature wooden bench at the end. Plants would be on either side of the path, the taller ones in the back, graduated to ground-hugging midgets toward the edges of the path.

ILLUSTRATION 113. *Identification sketch. 1. Azalea 'Gumpo.' 2.* Euonymus japonicus microphyllus variegatus. *3.* Echeveria glauca. *4.* Oxalis hedysaroides rubra. *5.* Neanthe bella. *6.* Begonia medora. *7.* Polystichum tsus-simense. *8.* Saxifraga stolonifera. *9.* Ficus diversifolia. *10.* Acorus gramineus variegatus. *11.* Dracaena marginata. *12.* Fatshedera lizei. *13.* Malpighia coccigera. *14.* Osmanthus ilicifolius. *15. Kalanchoe 'Tom Thumb.' 16. Begonia 'China Doll.' 17.* Cryptanthus bivittatus minor. *18.* Hedera helix *'Glacier.' 19.* Sedum dasyphyllum. *20. Begonia 'Bow-Joe.' 21.* Hedera helix *'Pixie.' 22.* Sinningia pusilla. *23. Begonia 'China Doll.' 24.* Sempervivum pumilum. *25.* Saxifraga stolonifera tricolor. *26.* Hedera helix *'Pixie.' 27.* Sinningia pusilla. *28.* Selaginella kraussiana. *29. Begonia 'Bow-Joe.' 30.* Pellaea rotundifolia. *31.* Selaginella kraussiana.

The plants in this miniature woodland garden will thrive in moderate temperatures with 50 per cent or more relative humidity, and at least three or four hours of sunlight each day, except, perhaps, in the heat of summer when they will do well in a shady place. Judicious pruning will keep these dwarf plants to the right proportions. The soil used was a commercially packaged medium containing a quantity of humus, chipped charcoal, and sand. Since the baking pan has no drainage holes, the soil is kept just nicely moist at all times. It should never be drenched.

ILLUSTRATION 114. *Miniature Japanese dish garden.*

🍃 A Japanese Dish Garden (Illustration 114)

Shibui, the Japanese word for exquisiteness, inspired the serenely simple dish garden in Illustration 114. Here just a few plants leave plenty of empty space. The path of chalk-white stepping stones winds and curves, finally disappearing behind the hillock and trees. The muted charcoal and white shades of the gravel complement the plants and blend harmoniously with stones and container. The container is, of all things, the saucer for a $1.69 plastic pot!

The plant at left in the foreground is *Sedum multiceps*, sometimes called "little Joshua tree." The irislike plants, disappearing in the distance, are *Acorus gramineus variegatus*. The plant at right in the foreground is *Gasteria liliputana*, a miniature succulent. In the background, the tree-like plant on the left is *Costus igneus*, an easily-grown ginger. In the background, at right, *Dizygotheca (Aralia) elegantissima* contrasts its black-green, fine-cut foliage against the chartreuse-green of the costus. If one outgrows the others, remove it carefully, and replace with another kind of plant. Any of the plants in Chapter 11 suggested for use number 39a are suitable for a desert garden.

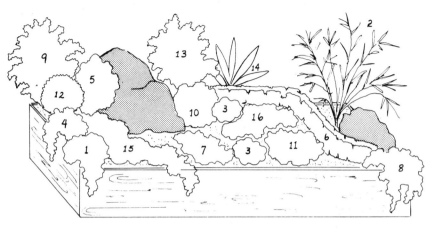

ILLUSTRATION 115. *A window sill landscape. 1.* Antirrhinun Asa-rina. *2.* Bambusa nana. *3.* Bellis perennis. *4.* Companula iso-phylla. *5.* Carissa grandiflora *'Boxwood beauty.' 6.* Euonymus japonicus microphyllus. *7. Felicia 'Sutton's Azure Blue.' 8.* Ficus pumila minima. *9.* Forsythia viridissima *var.* 'Bronxen-sis.'. *10.* Fragaria indica. *11.* Lobelia erinus pumila. *12.* Mal-pighia coccigera. *13.* Punica granatum nana. *14.* Scilla violacea. *15.* Thymus citriodorus aureus. *16. Torenia 'Gefion.'*

🌿 A Window-Sill Landscape (Illustration 115)

The garden shown in Illustration 115 has been designed for a window sill that receives at least four hours of direct sunlight each day in a temperature range of 50 to 72 degrees F. during fall, winter and spring. During the summer it could be left inside, or placed outside as a window box. This would be an excellent planting for a home greenhouse, also. The redwood box is 12 by 36 inches by 6 inches deep.

A planter box made of redwood to suit individual needs is suggested. A good planting medium for such a garden is equal parts topsoil, leaf mold, peat moss and clean, sharp sand. To plant, first spread about an inch of small pebbles or chipped charcoal over the bottom. Then fill to within an inch of the top with the soil mixture and put the plants in place.

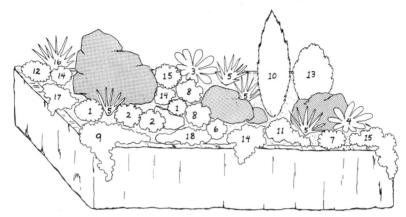

ILLUSTRATION 116. *A trough garden.* *1. Saxifraga 'Faldonside.'*
2. Saxifraga buseriana *'His Majesty.' 3.* Cyclamen coum. *4.*
Cyclamen neapolitanum. *5. Miniature narcissus. 6.* Gentiana
farreri. *7.* Primula allionii. *8.* Dianthus roysii. *9.* Androsace
lanuginosa leichtlinii. *10.* Juniperus communis compressa. *11.*
Androsace sempervivoides. *12.* Arabis sturii. *13. Azalea 'Gumpo.' 14.* Campanula betulaefolia. *15.* Campanula raineri. *16.*
Iris flavissima. *17. Phlox 'Ronsdorf Beauty.' 18.* Viola nana
compacta.

🌺 A Trough Garden (Illustration 116)

This planting has been designed for a cool, sunny greenhouse
or sun-heated pit. It can be summered either inside or out.
The actual landscape is contained in a "trough" or box made
of poured concrete. One of the delights of such a miniature
landscape is that it can be moved to different parts of the
house or garden for decoration, and is usually placed at table
height. If the concrete includes a lightweight aggregate such
as perlite or vermiculite, the container will be considerably
easier to move.

The garden shown in Illustration 116 is scaled for a container 2 by 3 feet by 7 inches deep. The size of a trough garden can be any that suits your individual need. The larger it
is, the more easily maintained since the soil does not dry out
quickly. However, size increases weight. A smaller trough,
about 12 by 20 inches, is more practical if one person must do
the lifting at moving time.

🌿 How To Make a Concrete Planter

To make a concrete planter box, you will need a wood surface on which to work, an outer and inner box the size of the trough you desire, reinforcing wire and cement, of course. There should be a drainage hole, and it is wise to gently slope the bottom of the container toward this. The area between the inner and outer box determines the thickness of the walls of the trough. These are usually an inch, or slightly more, in thickness. After the concrete has set, usually in about twenty-four hours, remove the forms. Then smooth off the sharp edges with a file. A stiff brush may be used to give the outside walls a smooth, attractive finish. The trough itself should not be moved until the concrete is completely dry.

🌿 Planting the Trough

Before a newly made concrete trough is planted, it should be soaked in a solution of permanganate of potash. The crystals of this should be added to water until it turns a dark, wine-red. Immerse the concrete container completely and allow it to soak for three days. If you have no container large enough, then put the potash solution directly inside the trough, stopping up the drainage hole beforehand. After the soaking period, wash the trough with clear water and leave it outdoors in the open for a week to ten days. Unless the weather provides rain, wash the trough daily with clear water.

A planting mixture of equal parts garden loam, peat moss, sand and leaf mold is excellent for most of the plants used in a trough garden. If individual plants have special preferences, however, it is possible to contain their soil mixture inside a sleeve of aluminum foil. This should have neither top nor bottom—just a tube to contain enough soil for the plant. The garden will benefit from the addition of a 3- or 4-inch potful of steamed bone meal mixed in with each bushel of soil mixture.

If you can get them, pieces of tufa stone make ideal accessories in a trough garden landscape. A product now available called Featherock, made of natural lava stone, is also useful for miniature gardens. It comes in two basic colors, both complementary to the landscape. These are silver-gray and charcoal.

When it comes to the actual planting, you will want to experiment with placement of stones, trees and plants. Once all are in final positions, and firmed into place, the surface of the entire garden should be covered with granite or limestone chippings. These help to keep the soil moist and cool during the summer. In addition, the chippings keep the crowns of alpines dry, and this is important because most of them dislike resting directly on damp soil.

HANGING BASKETS OF MINIATURE PLANTS

Diminutive plants that creep or climb are delightful when planted in hanging baskets. Your own artistic sense will guide you as to whether a basket will be prettier with one kind of plant, or whether it will be improved by the addition of others. The basic rule is to group plants that require the same or similar growing conditions. Illustration 117 shows a strawberry jar planted to tropicals, and suspended by small brass chains from a wall bracket. The plants in Illustration 118 require entirely different growing conditions, and none of them would be a good choice for combining in the same container with tropicals.

In addition to the plants illustrated in this chapter, any of those in Chapter 11 suggested for use number 38 are suited to planting in a suspended container.

Containers for Hanging Gardens

Hanging miniature gardens can be made in any small container that you might have in your kitchen or attic—or could find in an antique shop. For example, you might create a kitchen window garden of miniature hanging plants by placing them in a measuring cup, a soup ladle, a funnel and a

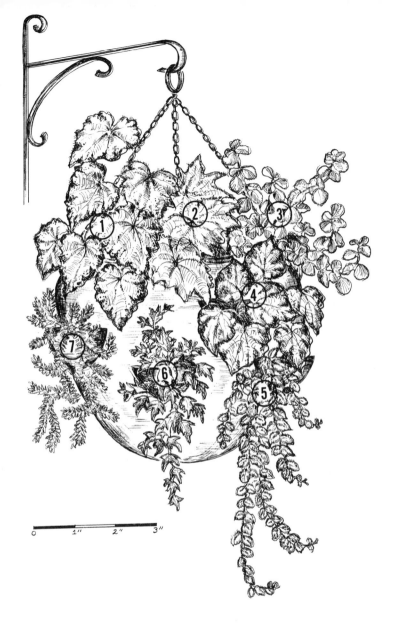

ILLUSTRATION 117. *Hanging garden—miniature plants in a strawberry-jar. 1.* Begonia bowerae. *2. Begonia 'Kathy Diane.' 3.* Pilea depressa. *4. Begonia 'China Doll.' 5.* Columnea microphylla. *6. Miniature ivy 'Needlepoint.' 7.* Selaginella kraussiana.

small gelatin mold. If the planter you choose has no drainage hole, then place a generous portion of charcoal in the bottom. This will help keep soil fresh. Be particularly careful in watering a basket that has no drainage hole. Keep the soil just nicely moist at all times. Avoid flood conditions and powdery dryness.

Almost all plants thrive in hanging baskets made of sphagnum moss. The basket form may be of wire and manufactured commercially. However, the smallest available is 8 inches in diameter. If you want smaller moss baskets, then you can make your own out of screen wire. When you have the basket molded to the size and shape desired, place the moss in it. Sphagnum for this purpose must be unmilled—as coarse as you can find. Spread and pack it all around the bottom and sides of the basket. Then make a liner of burlap or aluminum foil. This liner keeps the soil from draining through the sphagnum whenever the basket is watered, and thus it gives the planting longer life. If a foil liner is used, a few drainage holes should be punched in the bottom and lower part of the sides.

ILLUSTRATION 118. *Miniature plants in a coconut shell basket. Left to right:* Rhipsalis cereuscula, R. mesembryanthemoides *and* Hatiora salicorniodes.

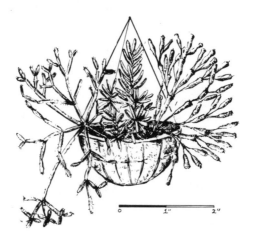

Consider the possibility of making tiny baskets, even less than 2 inches across, for use in terrariums and miniature landscapes. These can be constructed of redwood as true copies of large baskets, or of scraps of screen wire. Fill them with humus-rich soil that will retain moisture. Choose the tiniest of creepers for these baskets, and give them special care. Once established they will help create an enchanting miniature garden.

ILLUSTRATION 119. *A wall fountain of miniature plants. Left to right:* Sedum stahlii, Ceropegia woodii *and* Peperomia rubella.

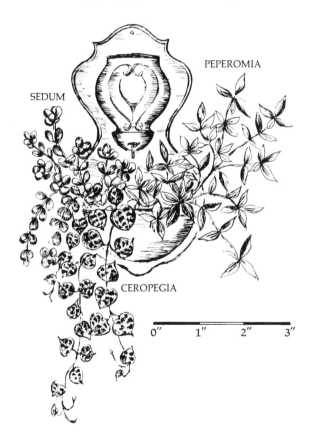

Appendix—Suppliers

Alberts & Merkel Bros., Inc., P.O. Box 537, Boynton Beach, Fla. 33435; orchids and other tropicals; catalog $1.

Alpenglow Gardens, 13328 King George Highway, Surrey, B.C. V3T236 Canada; alpines, evergreens, shrubs; catalog 25¢.

Annalee Violetry, 29-50 214th Place, Bayside, N.Y. 11360; African violets.

Brimfield Gardens Nursery, 245 Brimfield Rd., Wethersfield, Conn. 06109; dwarf evergreens.

John Brudy's Rare Plant House, P.O. Box 1348, Cocoa Beach, Fla. 32931; unusual seeds.

Buell's Greenhouses, Inc., P.O. Box 218, Weeks Road, Dept. HB4, Eastford, Conn. 06242; gesneriads; catalog 50¢.

Butcher, Thomas, Ltd., 60 Wickham Rd., Shirley, Croydon, Surrey CR98AG, England; seeds.

Carroll Gardens, Westminster, Md. 21157; dwarf evergreens.

Champion's African Violets, 8848 Van Hoesen Rd., Clay, N.Y. 13041; African violets.

Conrad-Pyle Star Roses, West Grove, Pa. 19390; miniature bush and tree roses.

Corliss Bros. Nursery, Essex Rd., Ipswich, Mass. 01938; dwarf evergreens.

Dauber's Nurseries, Rear 1705 N. George St., P.O. Box 1746, York, Pa. 17405; dwarf evergreens.

188

P. de Jager and Sons, Inc., 188 Asbury St., South Hamilton, Mass. 01982; daffodils, tulips, other bulbs.

Eastern Shore Nurseries, Inc., P.O. Box 743, Easton, Md. 21601; dwarf evergreens.

Fennell Orchid Co., 26715 S.W. 157th Ave., Homestead, Fla. 33030; orchids; catalog $1.

Fiori Enterprises, Prairie View, Ill. 60069; dwarf evergreens.

Girard Nurseries, P.O. Box 428, Geneva, Ohio 44041; dwarf evergreens.

Hillier and Sons, Winchester, England; alpines.

House Plant Corner, P.O. Box 810, Oxford, Md. 21654; supplies and equipment; catalog 25¢.

Margaret Ilgenfritz, Blossom Lane, Box 665, Monroe, Mich. 48161; orchids; catalog $2.

Jones and Scully, Inc., 2200 N.E. 33rd Ave., Miami, Fla. 33142; orchids; catalog $3.50.

Michael J. Kartuz, 92 Chestnut St., Wilmington, Mass. 01887; gesneriads, begonias; plants for growing under fluorescent light; catalog 50¢.

Logee's Greenhouses, 55 North St., Danielson, Conn. 06239; begonias, geraniums, other miniatures; catalog $1.

Lyndon Lyon, 14 Mutchler St., Dolgeville, N.Y. 13329; African violets and other gesneriads.

Mary-Ray Violets, 5007 Terry Dr., Alton, Ill. 62002; African violets.

Mayfair Nurseries, Rt. 2, Box 68, Nichols, N.Y. 13812; dwarf evergreens.

Rod McLellan Co., 1450 El Camino Real, S. San Francisco, Calif. 94080; orchids and supplies; catalog $1.

Merry Gardens, Camden, Maine 04843; begonias, geraniums, ivies, other miniatures; catalog $1.

Mini-Roses, P.O. Box 245 Station A, Dallas, Tex. 75208; miniature roses.

Oliver Nurseries, 1159 Bronson Rd., Fairfield, Conn. 06430; dwarf evergreens.

Palette Gardens, 26 W. Zion Hill Rd., Quakertown, Pa. 18951; dwarf evergreens.

George W. Park Seed Co., Inc., Greenwood, S.C. 29647; seeds, supplies, equipment.

Raraflora, 1195 Stump Rd., Feasterville, Pa. 19047; dwarf evergreens.

Sequoia Nursery, 2519 E. Noble, Visalia, Calif. 93277; miniature bush, tree, climbing, and hanging basket roses.

Sky-Cleft Gardens, Camp St. Extension, Barre, Vt. 05641; alpines.

Joel W. Spingarn, 1535 Forest Ave., Baldwin, N.Y. 11510; dwarf evergreens.

Fred A. Stewart, Inc., 1212 East Las Tunas Dr., P.O. Box 307, San Gabriel, Calif. 91778; orchids.

Sutton and Sons, Ltd., Reading, RG61AB England; seeds.

Thompson & Morgan, Ltd., Ipswich, England; seeds.

Tinari Greenhouses, 2325 Valley Rd., Box 190, Huntingdon Valley, Pa. 19006; African violets; catalog 25¢.

W. J. Unwin, Ltd., Southampton, England; seeds.

Index

(Plants in Chapter 11 are not included)

African violets, 7, 16-25, 174, 175
  food for, 17, 19
  humidity, 21
  isolation of, 17
  lights, 20-21
  pots for, 17, 19-20
  propagation of, 21-22
  soil for, 17
  temperature for, 20
  varieties of, 22-23, 25
  wick watering of, 19
American Orchid Society, 72

Begonias, 7, 26-37, 174-175
  growing conditions, 27
  propagation of, 27-28
  varieties of, 28-37
Black Magic African Violet Mix, 51
Bonsai, 46
Bottle garden, 13
Bulbs, *see* also individual plant names
  crocus, 38, 44
  forcing, 38-40
  hyacinth, 38, 45
  snowdrops, 45

City apartment garden, 8-9
Cold frame, 93, 100, 115
  for forcing, 39-40
Concrete planter, how to make, 183
Conifers, *see* Evergreens
Containers for miniature plants, 12, 22, 90, 170-171
  crystal, 174-175
  hanging baskets, 140, 184
  sphagnum baskets, 186

Daffodils, 38-42
  forcing, 38-40
  varieties of, 40-42
Dormancy, 12, 85-86

Evergreens, 8, 46-49
  varieties of, 47-49

Fertilizers, 10, 12, 27, 52, 63-64, 87, 101
Fluorescent lights, 7, 12, 13, 16, 20-21, 26, 38, 50-51, 52, 75, 84-85, 159, 163

Geraniums, 50-61, 63
  miniatures in tree form, 53
  pots for, 51
  promoting flowers in, 52-53
  propagating, 52
  shipping, 54
  soil for, 50-51
  varieties of, 54-61
Gesneriads, 9, 15, 16
Gloxinias, 9-10, 13, 16
  varieties of, 13-15
  see also *Sinningia pusilla*
Greenhouses, 12, 26-27, 39, 50, 64, 77, 93, 98, 99, 114, 115, 134
Growing mediums
  charcoal, 17, 22, 78, 179, 180, 186
  Cornell mix, 17
  G-B-S Growing Mix, 10, 27, 28, 175
  humus, 10
  osmunda fiber, 71, 102, 113
  for orchids, 73, 75, 76, 77, 78, 79, 80, 81, 82
  peat moss, 10, 28, 38, 39, 98, 100, 104, 106, 110, 116, 181, 183
  perlite, 10, 17, 38, 64, 65, 182
  soils, 17, 27, 50-51, 63, 64-65, 179
  sphagnum moss, 10, 11, 63, 64, 65, 73, 78, 115, 186
  UCLA mix, 17
  vermiculite, 10, 17, 21, 182

Hedera, see Ivy
Humidifier, 21

Insects, 65, 87-88, 177
Ivy, English (*hedera*), 7, 62-70, 175
  dimorphism in, 62
  how to grow, 64-65
  origin of new varieties, 63
  propagation of, 65-66
  tree form, 63
  varieties of, 66-70

Landscapes, miniature, 120, 176
  desert, 176-177
  Japanese dishgarden, 180
  trough, 182
  windowsill, 181
  woodland, 179
Limestone, 10, 114, 153
Lysol, 20

Mildew, 20, 54, 87

Narcissus, *see* Daffodil

Orchids, 71-83, 175
  insects on, 74
  light and temperature for, 74-75
  varieties of, 75-83

Peat moss, *see* Growing mediums
Perlite, *see* Growing mediums
Potting, 11, 19-20, 22

Roses
  containers for, 90
  culture in summer, 88
  from seeds, 89

humidity for, 85
light for, 84-85
red spider mites, 87-88
shipping of, 85-86
uses for, 90
ventilation of, 87
where to obtain, 85

Saintpaulias, 10, 16, *see* also African
  violets
Sinningia pusilla, 7, 9-15
  growing medium for, 10-11
  pots for, 9
  seeds, 11-12
  where to grow, 12
Sphagnum moss, *see* Growing mediums

Terrariums, 7-8, 12, 22, 27, 28, 29, 30,
  32, 34, 72, 78, 85, 175-176
Tulips, 38, 43

Vermiculite, *see* Growing mediums

Window gardens, 8, 16, 50, 64, 84,
  89-90